Fostering Now

Messages from Research

Ian Sinclair

Foreword by Tom Jeffrey,
Director General, Children, Young People and Families
Directorate, Department for Education and Skills

Jessica Kingsley Publishers
London and Philadelphia

First published in 2005
by Jessica Kingsley Publishers
116 Pentonville Road
London N1 9JB, UK
and
400 Market Street, Suite 400
Philadelphia, PA 19106, USA

www.jkp.com

Library of Congress Cataloging in Publication Data
Sinclair, Ian, 1938-
  Fostering now : messages from research / Ian Sinclair.-- 1st American paperback ed.
      p. cm.
  Includes bibliographical references and index.
  ISBN-13: 978-1-84310-362-2
1. Foster parents. 2. Foster children. 3. Foster home care. I. Title.
  HQ759.7.S55 2005
  362.73'3--dc22

2005004558

British Library Cataloguing in Publication Data
A CIP catalogue record for this book is available from the British Library

ISBN 978 1 84310 362 2

Contents

Foreword

Central and local government and the voluntary sector are working together to improve the lives of children, young people and families. *Every Child Matters: Change for Children* sets out the national framework to build services around the needs of children, young people and families. It has a strong emphasis on listening to children and other users in planning and developing services.

There is a particular concern about the need to improve outcomes for looked-after children. To support this aim, *Choice Protects* is delivering a major programme to improve the commissioning and delivery of foster care services.

This book gives an overview of current research in foster care. Drawing mainly on recent studies funded by the Department of Health, it is primarily concerned with what foster children want and what may work for them. These questions must be the starting point for any discussion of foster care. The book also illustrates the dedication of foster carers and explores the support they need.

This research will be of interest to all those involved in foster care. Much of the evidence confirms and reinforces existing beliefs, whilst some findings are challenging and surprising. We all share the task of considering the implications for practice.

This research contributes to the partnership between policy makers and those who work for children. All are committed to the welfare of children. By using knowledge about 'what works', we can transform this commitment into real improvements in outcomes.

Tom Jeffrey, Director General,
Children, Young People and Families Directorate,
Department for Education and Skills

Acknowledgements

Responsibility for this book lies with its author. Much of the work, however, has fallen to the advisory and implementation group. Their part in the process is described in 'The Overview Process': the quality of their diligent and constructive contributions should be acknowledged here. Particular recognition is due to Celia Atherton, who effectively recruited, administered and led the group, and Carolyn Davies, the group's Chair, who has played a key role in keeping alive the idea of overviews of this kind.

Outside the group the researchers on whose work the review is based willingly summarised their studies and constructively criticised a draft of the manuscript. Undoubtedly they improved it. So too did the foster children, the parents of foster children, foster carers, social workers, social work managers and elected members who, as part of the review process, were consulted about its messages.

More widely the studies themselves depended on foster children, their families, foster carers, adoptive parents, social workers and others in social services. Without their involvement the research could not have taken place. The book rests on the commitment, the understanding and the often deep feelings of thousands of people. An attempt has been made to make sense of their experience. It is hoped that others can build upon it.

The Overview Process

For many years non-technical summaries of research programmes and initiatives funded by the Department of Health's Children's Social Care section have been produced. The intention is to make the messages of research useful and intelligible to policy makers, service providers and practitioners. This particular summary has been completed after the transfer of the Department of Health's responsibilities for children's social care to the Department for Education and Skills. The studies themselves were almost all carried out before this transfer.

In keeping with earlier tradition the review has been written by an outside academic (Ian Sinclair) who has had available the advice of an outside 'advisory and implementation group', which consisted of practitioners, managers and others with expertise in foster care. The advisory implementation group saw the production of the report as one key element in a rather larger exercise, one that involved the various 'stakeholders' in foster care, the research community and others specifically concerned with training and dissemination. The key aim was to bring to a wider audience material that was relevant, evidenced and accessible.

In order to ensure relevance each study was read by two or more members of the advisory implementation group who contributed both a summary of the report and an assessment of its main implications. Members of the group also took responsibility for consulting with different groups of stakeholders (foster children, care leavers, their families, the children's own parents,* elected members and managers, social workers and other professionals) on the recommendations that were made. Ian Sinclair then drafted the overall report on the basis of this material and his own reading. The report was then critically read by the advisory implementation group as a whole. In order to ensure accuracy the researchers involved in the core studies also read the resulting draft report to ensure that their own work was properly represented and contributed the summaries of this work that are reproduced at the end. Ian Sinclair then took final responsibility for redrafting the report as a whole.

The assumption was that the report would not reach all those to whom it was relevant. The organisation Research in Practice took responsibility for developing

---

* In general, we use the word 'parents' for the children's own parents but 'birth parents' where it is important to distinguish between these and adoptive parents. Occasionally, for the sake of clarity or emphasis we use 'birth parents' even when the children are fostered.

six different leaflets variously aimed at elected members, foster children, their families, relative foster carers, unrelated foster carers, and professionals such as social workers. These leaflets were intended to bring key messages to the relevant group and also to act as an introduction to the research. They are available individually and as a set accompanying a video CD (*Fostering Voices*) which gives voice to the principal stakeholders in fostering: foster children, their families and foster carers. All these materials are available from the Department for Education and Skills (DfES) at the website *www.dfes.gov.uk/choiceprotects*.

In a further attempt to ensure that the report was widely accessible, two members of the implementation group, Ronny Flynn and Mary Day, worked with trainers to develop appropriate training exercises based on the report. This material can again be accessed at *www.dfes.gov.uk/choiceprotects*.

Chapter 1

Introducing the Report

The cumulative evidence of these…reports is weighty and convincing… Virtually all the findings point in the same direction. As one member of the practitioners' group put it, reading these reports is like looking out of different windows and seeing the same view.

(Rowe *et al.*, p.5[24])

Introduction

At any one time English local authorities look after around 60,000 children and young people. Around two thirds of this number are fostered. This report brings together 16 research studies that have been primarily concerned with these foster children or their carers. Taken together these studies should provide a better-founded and wider base for policy and practice than any individual study on its own. All but three were commissioned by the Department of Health, whose continuing responsibilities for the research have now been taken over by the Department for Education and Skills (DfES). Why were they commissioned? What did they cover? What does the report seek to do with them?

The policy and research background to the studies

The studies began against a background of concern about the care system in general and foster care in particular. The Government initiatives known as 'Quality Protects' and 'Choice Protects' showed a new urgency in their approach to the problems of the care system and a new emphasis on its outcomes. Foster care itself was seen by some as being 'in crisis'. In the introductions to their studies the various researchers identify the challenges currently faced by foster care and do so in very similar ways.

First, the population in foster care is not the same as it was in the past. In comparison with the early 1980s children now are much less likely to enter the care system because of parental misfortune or simply because of their own truancy or trouble with the law. The proportion entering because they are abused has been growing steadily, while, among teenagers, a difficulty in getting on with their family remains important. Taken as a whole children looked after now almost certainly pose greater challenges to their carers than was once the case.

In the case of foster care these challenges have been increased by changes in residential care and adoption. Over the past 20 years the number of children in residential homes has dropped dramatically. More recently there have been determined efforts to increase the number of very young children who are adopted. Despite these changes the number of children looked after by foster carers has increased. As a result foster carers are looking after a much higher proportion of children in the care system than they once did. Fewer children are likely to enter a foster home when very young and spend the rest of their childhood there. However, many who are now fostered would once have been in residential care.

A second key issue arises from a changed view of the role of foster carers. Foster carers are no longer described as 'foster parents' who bring children up as they do 'their own'. Instead they are expected to work in tandem with the foster children's own parents who have 'parental responsibility'. Children have a right to a family life and, other things being equal, a right to regular contact with their families. These new expectations, the development of Fostering Network (formerly the National Foster Care Association) and the growth of special schemes for professional fostering have all led to a demand for a more professional role and greater professional status for foster carers. At the same time the aspirations to professional status have not been accompanied by the widespread adoption of professional pay and professional training for foster carers.

The third issue arises from a general acceptance that there are not enough carers to fill these new roles. This is partly explained by pointing to changes in wider society. More women take paid work outside the home, the period of their life which they devote exclusively to child rearing has reduced, more have responsibilities for ageing parents, more have to look after children without the support of a partner. All these reasons reduce the pool of women from which foster carers have traditionally been recruited. The independent 'for profit' sector has responded to this challenge by offering enhanced remuneration and support. Its rapid growth presents a challenge to local authorities seeking to recruit new carers and retain old ones.

This situation has produced a number of pressures on foster care. These include:

- a lack of a widely accepted theory appropriate to foster care, which has sometimes been seen as something which carers do 'by the light of nature'

- a lack of choice of foster placements – this has been particularly acute for certain groups of foster children: disabled children, teenagers, sibling groups and black and Asian children

- the exacerbation of previous stresses on foster carers arising from the difficulties posed by taking into their house children who have often been abused, who may accuse them of abuse and whose parents may find the situation difficult but who nevertheless have to be made welcome

- a tension between the needs of foster children for a 'professional approach' based on an understanding of their difficulties with a need in many cases for long-term care with an opportunity to stay with their carers until they are adults

- a lack of attention to long-term foster care as opposed to the more highly valued adoption.

These issues are highly relevant to the findings of the core studies and they apply now as they did at the time of the research.

At the same time policy and practice has inevitably developed since the research was commissioned. On the one hand there have been major developments concerned with the well-being of large numbers of potentially disadvantaged children – Sure Start or, at the other end of the age range, Connexions are clear examples of this trend. On the other hand there has been an increasingly sharp focus on the challenges faced by the comparatively small number of children looked after in the care system. There has been a particular concern that these children and young people should have much greater stability in their lives, that as many as possible should have the chance to grow up in a supportive family environment and that outcomes for this group should be dramatically improved across the board.

Progress is being made. We have seen new legislation – including the Care Standards Act 2000, the Children (Leaving Care) Act 2000 and the Adoption and Children Act 2002 – the wider adoption reform programme, the Choice Protects initiative and the use of targets and change agents to drive up performance and share good practice.

A cross-cutting trend has been the emphasis on 'joining up' services. This can be seen both in services designed for large groups of children and young people (for example the Connexions service) and in the greatly increased emphasis on the health and education of young people who are looked after and on care leavers. The development of multidisciplinary teams involving different combinations of professional expertise is a further example. Most recently we have seen the publication in 2003 of *Every Child Matters* (Cm 5860) setting out the Government's vision for the development of children's services, and the introduction of the Children Bill to create the necessary legislative base to realise that vision.

It is tempting to feel that these new developments render the research out of date. This would be a mistake. The underlying issues are unlikely to change. What is important is that an effort is made to relate the research messages to the new opportunities. For example, there is evidence that carers were reluctant to adopt because of the loss of financial and other forms of support this would involve. It is important to consider how far similar constraints may apply in the case of the new Special Guardianship. Similarly there have been developments in setting and monitoring standards. These do not invalidate earlier findings and may be informed by them.

What are the core studies?

The studies were selected on three grounds:

- All have been published or completed since 1998.
- All had as a key focus foster carers, foster placements or the consequences of fostering for children and carers.
- With three exceptions, all were commissioned by the Department of Health.

The decision to focus on Department of Health studies reflects the funding of the review. The department has a tradition of summarising its research programmes and developing recommendations on the back of them. Three studies were commissioned by the then Scottish Office. These were so relevant to the themes of the others that it seemed wrong to leave them out. Others could have been included on similar grounds. It was, nevertheless, necessary to draw a line, however arbitrary, at some point. Otherwise it would have been necessary to include all the research on foster care.

We give details of the samples, design and main conclusions of the 16 core studies in Appendix A. The present chapter names the studies and gives the briefest of details about them. In this way the reader should be able to carry them in mind. The superscript number given for each study is that used to reference it. Full bibliographic information is provided in the References section at the end of the book, and the superscript numbers correspond to each work's place in that section.

- Shared care study (Aldgate and Bradley)[1] – an intensive study of 60 children and their families who were involved in shared care schemes in four different parts of the country and followed up over periods of six to nine months.

- Contact study (Cleaver)[2] – a retrospective file study of the first 'care episode' of 152 children in 6 authorities and a prospective 1-year study of 33 children aged 5 to 12.

- Adolescent fostering study (Farmer, Moyers and Lipscombe)[3] – a follow-up study of 68 children aged 11 to 17 who were studied 3 months and 12 months into placement.

- Review of care by relatives (Hunt)[4] – a literature review of research on foster care provided by family and friends.

- Remuneration and performance study (Kirton, Beecham and Ogilvie)[5] – a study using available data on all English authorities and a large postal survey of carers (n = 1181), focus groups and interviews in 16 authorities and five independent fostering agencies (IFAs).

- Training study (Macdonald and Kakavelakis)[6] – a random controlled trial of training using a mainly behavioural approach and coming to mainly negative conclusions about the impact of the training.

- Long-stay placement study (Quinton, Rushton, Dance and Mayes)[7] – a follow-up study of 61 children who were studied 1 and 12 months into intended long-stay placements which were mainly but not exclusively adoptive.

- Sibling study (Rushton, Dance, Quinton and Mayes)[8] – a study of 133 children placed long term for adoption or fostering and studied 3 and 12 months after placement.

- Adoption study (Selwyn, Sturgess, Quinton and Baxter)[9] – a four- to ten-year follow-up of 130 children who had been subject to a best interests decision that they should be placed for adoption. The study compares the careers and outcomes of those found to be stably adopted, stably looked after, or unstably looked after.

- York studies (Sinclair, Wilson, Baker and Gibbs) – three linked studies involving (a) an 18-month follow-up of 1528 foster carers, 940 of whom returned a detailed questionnaire, and (b) 14- and 36-month follow-ups of 596 children fostered with these carers. The reports focus on carers,[10] placements[11] and the three-year follow-up.[12]

- Loughborough consumer study (Skuse and Ward)[13] – a qualitative interview study of 49 children who had ceased to be looked after and half of whom were followed up for a second interview.

- East Anglia study (Thoburn, Norford, Charles, Parvez Rashid and Moffatt)[14] – a study of 297 minority ethnic children who were placed for adoption or long-term fostering between 1979 and 1986 and followed up for periods of between 12 and 15 years.

- Triseliotis study (Triseliotis, Walker and Hill)[15] – a study of 822 active foster carers and 96 former carers and of the organisations in which they worked.

- CAPS or specialist fostering study (Walker, Hill and Triseliotis)[16] – a longitudinal study of 20 young people aged 9 to 17 who were placed in a specialist scheme intended as an alternative to secure provision.

In selecting these studies we are conscious of omitting others which were also funded by the Department of Health and which also have valuable comments to make on foster care. Among these we have made particular use of studies by Farmer and Moyers,[17] Farmer and Pollock,[18] Harwin et al.,[19] Lowe et al.,[20] Packman and Hall[21] and Ward et al.[22] (again, superscript numbers correspond to the works' position in the References section at the end of this book). These studies were not included in the 'core set' because they are as yet unfinished,[17] or because they concentrated specifically on sexual abuse[18] or on more general issues in the care system such as delay and the processes through which decisions were made.[19,20,21,22] We have used data from these studies in particular parts of the report. We have not, however, used them throughout the book and they are not summarised in their own right at the end.

The core studies themselves include three general studies of all foster carers,[5,10,15] two linked follow-up studies[11,12] of a large sample of all foster children in placement at a particular point and a qualitative study[13] of formerly looked-after children of varying ages. The remaining studies have a more specialist focus either in terms of age group, or issue (e.g. contact, training, remuneration, specialist fostering) or both.

In general the authors of the studies seek to describe the various samples, to understand the processes involved through interviews and similar methods, and to relate both sample characteristics and processes to outcomes. The existence of some general studies and other more specialised ones means that the studies complement each other. They are stronger as a group than any would be on their own. That said, the studies have, as discussed below, some limitations.

How confident can we be about the conclusions?

One point should be made very strongly at the outset. With the exception of one study,[1] which considered shared care, the studies dealt almost exclusively with longer-staying children who were looked after for at least six months. These foster children now make up around 85 per cent of those who are looked after at any one time. However, more than 40 per cent of those who cease to be looked after during a year have been 'in care' for less than six months. The conclusions we reach may be relevant to this 'short-term group'. They cannot, however, automatically be held to apply to them. This is particularly true of conclusions we reach about 'going home' and 'contact'. Similar reservations apply to private fostering. None of the studies considered it and this report does not either.

A second key limitation of these studies lies in the absence from many of them of the views of parents, and particularly of fathers. These views are represented in some studies (e.g. the contact study[2] and York study 3[12]). However, they are not as much a focus as are the views of foster children and carers. This omission should be kept in mind in considering the balance of the report.

A third key limitation lies in the difficulty of giving an adequate account of the influence of ethnicity. Ethnic monitoring did not become a requirement for local authorities until 2000, and although many had been keeping records for years, practice nationally was patchy. Against this background the numbers of children from minority ethnic groups was, in most studies, small. Statistical analysis in these studies was, if possible at all, only practicable on the basis of grouping together children who might have little in common apart from the fact that they were not 'white British'. Again, this is an area where research practice will need to become more sophisticated.

In general the core studies have variously relied on:

- the views of foster children, social workers, foster carers and parents

- other descriptive data (e.g. on the ages of foster carers and their families' composition)

- statistical assessment of the impact of different factors on outcomes, usually after allowing for the effects of other variables (e.g. the effect of foster carers on 'breakdowns' after allowing for the fact that some carers have 'easier' foster children)

- experimental manipulation – the provision of training to a randomly selected group of carers whose outcomes are compared with those achieved by a group selected using the same random process but not given training

- judgements made by the researchers (often themselves experienced social workers) on the basis of case material and other data.

None of these sources of evidence is free of difficulty. Foster children's views are important in their own right and often provide vital insights. Social workers, foster carers and parents all have important things to say but neither they, the foster children nor the researchers have infallible judgement. Statistical explanations of outcome are important – but it is always possible that key variables have not been taken into account. Even experiments leave open the question of exactly what are the key ingredients in ensuring that an approach did or did not work. This, along with the difficulty of getting adequate numbers, often makes it difficult to use the results as a basis for predicting the future.

In practice, judgements about the conclusions can only partly be based on the quality of evidence in the individual studies (e.g. size of sample, and reliability of measures). Four additional considerations are very important:

- *Common probability* – how likely are the conclusions, working on the basis of professional opinion, previous research and relevant theory?

- *Calculated probability* – are the differences discussed large enough and the numbers great enough to make it very unlikely that they occur 'by chance'?

- *Coherence* – how far do the different studies arrive at similar conclusions and how far do the different sources of evidence (e.g. children's views and statistical data) support each other?

- *Consequences* – what are the practical risks of accepting a conclusion when it is wrong as against rejecting it when it is right?

The last point may need an example to illustrate it. Some studies found that carers who said they had received insufficient information on a child were more likely to have a placement breakdown. This could represent cause and effect. This situation could also arise because carers were only likely to report inadequate information if they had had a nasty surprise. In practice most would agree that carers should be given full information as far as possible. There is little practical risk in accepting that this will also reduce placement breakdown. In contrast, there *are* risks in accepting the apparent implications of some of the findings on contact.

Very similar points can be made about the difficulties of making recommendations. These are based on research findings. For example, children in a number of studies complain about the practice of seeking social work permission before they are allowed to sleep in their friend's houses overnight. A natural corollary is that foster carers should be allowed to grant these permissions and also others (e.g. undertaking risky sports, going on school trips). The argument, however, is not watertight. To proceed in this way might make the children less safe, undermine parents, make foster carers liable to pressure from the children and law suits from parents and so on.

Our recommendations are based on weighing such conflicting considerations. The reader is asked to do the same. Research assists judgement. It is not a substitute for it.

How does this report relate to other research?

There are numerous studies of foster care, many of them carried out in the United States. How does this report relate to these other sources of knowledge? Part of the answer can be seen by comparing the present report with one which was recently written for the Social Care Institute of Excellence (SCIE) and which did review US research along with research produced in Britain.[23]

Comparison of the two reports suggests many similarities. Both conclude that many children do better in foster care than they would do if they were at home. Both identify the same group of factors as determining outcomes within foster care. The broad recommendations are much the same. These similarities are not surprising. The academic who wrote this book also worked on the SCIE report. Most of the research summarised in this report was also available when the previous report was written and so informed its conclusions.

At the same time there are differences. This report is about a programme of British research. It is therefore easier to conclude that its findings are relevant to a British audience. As the report deals with a smaller number of studies, it is possible to consider these studies in much more detail. The advisory panel has reviewed each chapter of the report in order to derive more specific suggestions and recommendations.

The two reports are therefore complementary. The SCIE report provides reassurance that the conclusions of the British research reviewed here are indeed compatible with the broad sweep of international research. In this respect it also complements a paper by Hunt[4] who has recently completed a review of the international research on foster care by 'kin'. In contrast, the present report takes the opportunity to review a small number of studies in more depth and to make detailed suggestions for British practice.

How have we written up the results?

The reports provide material on the basic dilemmas raised by foster care and on possible ways forward. On the evidence of the studies reviewed, foster care is a very impressive form of provision. At the same time it offers a basic dilemma. It rarely provides very long stays in the same family and it may fail either to change the situations from which foster children come or to offer a permanent alternative to them.

Solutions to this dilemma involve the recruitment and retention of more carers, including more who, from the start, plan to care for the child placed with them as permanent members of their family, the development of yet more effective placements, along with enhanced attention to education and the development of practice with parents. They may also require changes in the role that the system plays and the theory that underpins it. These are the issues covered in the report.

In the report we seek to make the basis for what we say as clear as possible. Undoubtedly some busy people will read or skim our report and not read the original material; we hope that most will go to the studies themselves. These give more thorough accounts of the research than is possible in a summary. Almost all of them provide detailed case material. This qualitative material has provided the source for the quotations at the beginning of the chapters. In general, however, it cannot be easily summarised even though it does provide invaluable insights into foster care. This is a rich set of studies that has taken much time and trouble to produce. Those in the field should make as much use of this material as time allows.

One final, but very important, point concerns a danger in the report. Foster children have been through troubling experiences. As a consequence some of them behave in ways which others find difficult. They are then labelled as 'hyperactive' or 'disturbed', or as suffering from 'attachment disorder' or some other problem. Researchers and psychologists create ways of measuring these attributes. Foster children may then be seen in ways they do not recognise, discussed in terms they would not accept and treated as members of a difficult group rather than as individuals in their own right. The danger is that the report encourages others to see and treat foster children in this way.

This danger cannot be avoided. Any adjective – brave, clever, stupid – groups, labels and separates out individuals. Where labels are intended to demean they are clearly hurtful: more should be done in checking with children and young people what language they find offensive. Nevertheless, those planning services and training need these labels. If, for example, it is true that many foster children are likely to suffer from an identifiable 'attachment disorder' it is presumably important that foster carers have the training to respond sensitively to this.

There are, however, other points to be made. First, foster children are enormously varied. Absolutely nothing, except perhaps the facts that they are human and children, is true of all of them. It is therefore very important that those dealing with an individual child approach them without firm presuppositions. They can bear in mind that a foster child is, for example, likely to have complex feelings about loss; they should not assume that this is necessarily true.

Second, labels are not explanations. They are a poor guide to the way those labelled experience the world. Children who follow their foster carer around may be labelled as suffering from 'anxious attachment'. This is not a precise explanation of why an individual child behaves in this way. It passes over the fact that he or she may (or may not) feel unbearably lonely.

So this report is written with the recognition that research inevitably classifies and labels. Commonly it seems to treat individuals as 'objects'. Despite this it can be of use in the world of purposes and feelings. The task for the reader is to make creative use of the findings without treating them as more than they are.

Chapter 2

Home or Away? Some Basic Issues

I think Samantha's mum, I don't know much about her, but I think she was a very damaged person too, but she loved her daughter, I'm quite sure of it, in her own way. (Foster carer)

I had been fighting for her to come back…but…the day she come back to me, I think they put me, locked me in prison and threw away the key… I told her the other day…'I feel as though I am on a life support machine, just lifeless, nothing there…'cos you took everything away from me.' (Samantha's mother)

If they'd have said to you 'We've got a family that's interested in adopting you or something like that?'
Oh no, no.
But why would that have been a 'no no'?
'Cos it just would. I wouldn't be able to see my mum. I'd flip if they offered me adoption. I'd flip so. (Samantha, a foster child, and interviewer)

Introduction

Most children who are looked after return home. Recent figures suggest that four in ten (43%) cease to be looked after within six months of starting. Thereafter the likelihood of returning home in the near future drops rapidly. Nevertheless it never vanishes. So there is a steady trickle of children returning to their families. In the end a majority probably go home, although many do not stay there long.[12]

Whether or not children return home, their subsequent lives are often difficult. They are less likely than others to achieve educationally, more likely to suffer from mental ill health, and more likely to be homeless or in prison.[23] Some see these difficulties as caused by the care system. Others argue that the children's behavioural and other difficulties existed before they were looked after. Indeed there is evidence that younger children who stay looked after may have better mental and physical health than those who return home.[23] Children who continue for some time in the care system are less likely to get into trouble with the police and more likely to thrive in a variety of ways than those who spend a shorter time or return home.[23]

This evidence raises a number of important questions:

- Should children be removed from home more often, less often, or for longer or shorter periods of time?
- What does this imply about the kinds of provision that should be available?
- What principles should govern this provision?
- How should these principles be embodied in the day-to-day practice of foster care?

The report considers all these questions. This particular chapter considers the first of them: the question of whether children should be looked after away from home. A variety of findings are relevant. These concern:

- the reasons for which the children are looked after
- the children's views on returning home
- how far their parents want them back
- their likelihood of returning home
- the outcomes of those who return home and of those who do not
- the degree to which the looked-after system seems able to provide the children with a satisfactory, stable alternative to returning home
- the degree to which other long-term options, such as adoption or Special Guardianship (at the time residence orders), provide a better option than foster care.

We will look at these issues in turn.

Reasons for being looked after

It is well known that children who have contact with social services come overwhelmingly from families who are poor and disadvantaged in terms of social class.[23] The studies make it clear that foster children face additional difficulties before they enter the care system. These difficulties have usually been apparent to social services and are often of long standing. Cleaver, for example, found that 86 per cent of children were already known to social workers and in half the cases they were known for more than two years before admission.[2] Exact figures differ between studies but all make the following points:

- Very few children had been living with both parents. Most commonly they had been living with their mother on her own or with a stepfather.

- In all but the shared care study[1] between 50 per cent[14] and 90 per cent[9] of the children had been abused (proportions which some researchers saw as an underestimate).

- Older children were less likely than younger ones to be looked after for reasons explicitly connected with abuse – other factors that increase the likelihood of being looked after, such as the child's behaviour and breakdown of family relationships,[3,13] were also quite common in this group.

- All groups had nevertheless experienced high levels of family adversity (domestic violence, multiple moves, severe deprivation).[2,3,9]

- Older children in particular were likely to show challenging behaviour.[3,9,11,16] Behavioural problems were not, however, confined to this group. Nearly a third of the children in the short-term fostering study were described as displaying difficult behaviour while fostered.

These findings suggest that the children's situations were generally very serious. Those who are looked after for any length of time (the group largely considered in these studies) are not looked after for trivial reasons. It may be correspondingly difficult for them to return home. If they are to return, there needs to be adequate and effective support available to them.

The children's views of returning home

The children's views reflected this earlier history. They were certainly preoccupied with their relationships with their families. They had varying views about how close they wanted these to be. To judge from two of the York studies,[11,12] some wanted to be back with their families; others, to live with their foster carers and see their families often; others, to get on with their lives in foster care, perhaps be adopted by their carers, and see little if anything of their parents. On balance, however, most did not want to go home. Most foster children who replied to the York questionnaires wanted to stay where they were until they reached the age of at least 18 and, in a sizeable minority of cases, beyond this.

Children looking back on their time in the care system were equally appreciative. The Loughborough researchers[13] interviewed 49 children and young people who were no longer 'in care', 25 of them on two occasions. Around three quarters thought that it had been a good idea that they had been looked after. Care was not generally seen as the source of their poor school performance or other difficulties. Instead it was seen both as a solution to a serious problem and as a springboard, a place for 'getting one's act together', forming plans, improving education and so on. The best things about it were likely to be material provisions and opportunities, relationships with individual staff and social workers and the family environment provided by some foster carers.

These views are those of children looked after for some time – many short-term entrants are much more wary about 'care'.[20] Nevertheless, as already pointed out, most of those in the care system at any one time have spent a considerable period of time there.

Parents' views of return

Earlier research has suggested that parents' views of 'care' are complex. Feelings of shame, guilt and anger are commonly mixed with feelings of relief and, sometimes, a sense of having acted for the best.[23] Two of the core studies[2,3] point out that parents' attitudes reflect the reasons for care. Where this is defined as arising from parental request or the difficult behaviour of the child it can be welcomed. Where it is seen as 'compulsory' it is commonly resented. Other research[20,22] supports this conclusion but also suggests that parental attitudes towards 'care' may become less hostile over time.

Two studies point out the difficulty parents have in asking for help. Parents in Aldgate and Bradley's study[1] wanted relief care but they did not want the stigma and risk of losing their child that went with it. In one of the York studies[12] adoptive parents and the parents of former foster children expressed a very similar wariness over accepting help from social workers.

The likelihood of returning home

The likelihood of returning home obviously varied with the child's age and with the purpose of his or her placement. Only two children in the short breaks study were not able to continue at home.[1] Rates of return home among children recently placed in care from the community are known to be quite high. In contrast, hardly any of the children in the studies of long-stay placement returned home in the period covered by the research.[7,8,14] Older young people in foster care were more likely to go into independent living than to return home.[12,16]

Two studies[2,12] focused on children who were fostered for three months or more. The first suggested that about a third were believed to be at home after four years.[2] The other found that 27 per cent of the children returned home at some stage over three years. Many of these, however, then moved on. Only 17 per cent were living with their families at the three-year follow-up point.[12] The Loughborough study similarly found that many of those returning home did not remain there long.[13]

These studies therefore suggest a rough pattern. National figures suggest that about a third of those who start to be looked after cease to be so within three months. Most of these probably go home. A further third probably go home at least for a time within the next four years. More go home after this. How do those who return 'get on' in comparison to those who remain looked after?

The outcomes of those returning home and those remaining

Very little is known about the outcomes of those who go home after a brief time 'in care'. Earlier research suggests that compared with their peers they do not do well.[23] It is not known whether they would do better or worse if they remained looked after. The core studies provide more relevant information on those whose initial stay lasts longer.

One study,[13] based heavily on the children's views, paints a bleak picture of life after leaving care. Official support at this point was patchy. A quarter of the children had no contact with a social worker. Others reported support from social workers which focused on practical matters and tailed off (a finding consistent with the last York study[12]). Some valued relationships with foster carers with whom more than half had some further contact. However, few of these relationships appeared to provide a high degree of support.

The Loughborough study[13] suggested that children who had been adopted or placed with relatives on residence orders could be well supported. In contrast, older children returning home generally did not stay there and frequently lived with a wide variety of relatives. Care leavers often had numerous changes of housing. Contact with and support from relatives remained important but relationships were not necessarily good enough to enable child and parent to live together.

The consequences of this situation were apparent in a number of studies:

- Placements were commonly thought to come to an end too soon. In the short-term study children enjoying the placements could not see why they should stop.[1]

- Some returns home took place despite the child's poor attachment to the parents, erratic parental visits to the child and no change in the home situation. In some cases it was apparent that return would fail although it was precipitated by what the child wanted. Some returns home were clearly dangerous and potentially damaging for the child.[2,12]

- Returning home could work against stability in the longer term. In the adoptions study a quarter of the children returned home, sometimes at the instigation of the courts. Of these '81 per cent re-entered care within a matter of months (mean 14 weeks) following further abuse'.[9] Attempts at reunification were much more common among the group of children who, despite a 'best interests decision', went on to have highly unstable care careers.

- Longer-staying children who returned home at any stage were more likely to be re-abused, less likely to be rated as doing well at school and more likely to display a wide variety of difficult behaviours – differences that were not apparently explained by these children's earlier behaviour and difficulties while they were fostered.[12]

- A sizeable minority of carers and young people in the last York study felt their move to independence had taken place before they were ready.[12] Foster carers in the adoption study were very critical of the pressure they felt was placed on the young people to move on around the age of 16.[9] Only two of the completed placements in the Scottish study of treatment foster care were thought to have lasted as long as needed.

- Social workers and foster carers were much more likely to rate the placement as adequate and safe when the child was fostered or adopted than when he or she returned home or went into independent living.[12]

These problems need to be viewed in the context of the samples studied. By definition children who returned home at some point but went on to receive a 'best interests decision' did not succeed at home. The adoption sample could not contain examples of successful rehabilitation. Nevertheless other research also suggests that plans made for returning home quite commonly do not succeed.[19,20] Other qualitative research also suggests that some parents feel undermined by the higher standard of living on offer in foster care. It is not surprising that some had difficulty in coping, particularly given the generally low level of community support.[12,13]

For these reasons the findings are not a conclusive argument against attempts at rehabilitation. Many children and parents wanted to be together. These wishes have moral force.[19] The findings do point to the very serious risks involved in rehabilitation. Equally, however, it is important to look critically at the alternatives. How far can foster care offer a child a genuine family alternative to rehabilitation with family?

Can foster care offer a permanent alternative to care at home?

The most pervasive concern about the care system probably focuses on its instability.[19,20,21,22,23] This raises the question of whether long-stay foster care deprives a child of his or her home without providing an alternative permanent family.

The core studies leave no doubt that:

- foster care can provide long-term stable care in which children remain in contact with their foster family in adulthood.[9,14] This is particularly so when the placement is intended to be permanent from the start[14]

- for most children the care system did not provide this long-term stable alternative to care at home.[12] Even those placed 'long term' had commonly been moved frequently before placement[7,8,14]

- most long-stay foster children wanted to move less than they did. A minority, however, complained that they were not moved from places where they were unhappy[11]

- a small minority of children have very unstable care careers. Paradoxically, the more unsatisfactory the child's career the more it costs. Children with highly unstable careers may attract social services costs of over half a million pounds.[9]

The degree of stability varied by age. Children under the age of ten often spent a considerable period of time with the same carers[12] and the risk of breakdown among them was comparatively low.[2,7,8,12] In contrast, breakdowns occurred in around 40 to 50 per cent of teenage placements even when the placement had lasted some time and the period at risk was less than three years.[3,12,14] The study by Thoburn et al.[14] found no significant difference between broadly similar children placed at a late age for adoption and placed as 'permanent foster children'. They concluded that the main influences were the age and difficulty of the children.

In general there were very few children who spent long periods – say eight years or more – with the same family of carers. There were four main reasons for this:

- Authorities made determined efforts to return children home. If a child was less than two years old he or she almost always returned home or was adopted.[12]

- Efforts at rehabilitation did not always work out. Except in the shared care study[1] the proportion of children who had 'previously been in care' varied from 61 per cent[3] to 34 per cent.[13]

- The risk of breakdown was substantial, particularly during the teenage years.

- Very few children stayed on with their carers after the age of 18 and those that did generally did not stay long.[12]

The length of time that a child spent in placement did not always predict the quality of his or her relationship with carers. On the one hand breakdowns could occur without finally breaking the relationship. Some young people could only continue a relationship because they were no longer living with their carers.[14] Others renewed relationships with their carers in their twenties even though these had broken down in their teens.[14] On the other hand the absence of breakdown does not mean that the child or the carer is happy.[2,8] Most children did seem to feel that they belonged in the family. However, not all did and some children could feel they did not belong, even though their placement had lasted a long time.[12]

Against this background one study[12] distinguished between four different kinds of permanence:

- *Objective permanence* occurred if children had a placement which would last for their childhoods and would provide back-up and, if needed, accommodation after the age of 18.

- *Subjective permanence* occurred if the child felt he or she belonged in the family.

- *Enacted permanence* occurred if all concerned behaved as if the child was a family member (e.g. the child was included in family occasions).

- *Uncontested permanence* occurred if the child did not feel a clash of loyalties between foster and birth family.

In general it was apparent that foster care could provide long-term, quasi-adoptive placements. It was also clear that, for reasons to do with policy, practice and break-downs, it usually did not.

The acceptability and outcomes of other long-term options

The difficulty of returning foster children to their homes might suggest that they should be adopted. If so, evidence from two studies[9,12] suggests that the decision would have to be made early. In the adoption study 50 of the 130 children subject to a best interests decision were nevertheless not with adoptive parents at follow-up. The chance of not being adopted increased by 1.8 for every extra year of age at entry to care and by 1.6 for every subsequent year before the best interests decision was made.[9] Other studies also documented the very strong relationship between age and the likelihood of adoption.[12,19,20]

In the adoption study delays in achieving adoption arose in part from preventive work. Commonly this was not grounded in a full assessment and not sufficiently intensive or prolonged to mitigate the appalling circumstances in which the children lived. It was nevertheless often continued long after the point at which it was obvious that it was not working. For a minority of children (41%) the problem was then compounded by a failure to put in place a permanency plan within two years of entry to the care system.

Other research[19,20,22] has similarly documented the frequency with which failed efforts at rehabilitation, combined with the assumption that 'home is best', delay placement for adoption among young children. These studies point to the role of the courts in these failed attempts,[22] a failure by social workers to make a realistic assessment of parental capacity,[22] a lack of agreed times for reviewing attempts at rehabilitation,[20] and delays in the provision of drug and other adult services leading to delays in decisions.[22] One study found that looked-after babies whose mothers had experienced problems with drugs, alcohol misuse, domestic violence or mental health hardly ever returned home. This, however, did not mean that decisions about them were quickly taken.[22]

Two studies[9,12] suggested that on some criteria related to attachment adopted children improved more than those who remained in foster care. Undoubtedly they had more stability in their lives, but this result may partly reflect differences between those children who were adopted and others. The benefits may also have been restricted to those without severe and overlapping early adversities.[9]

Other studies, as well as those just mentioned, suggest that on place-ment-related criteria (e.g. breakdown and behavioural change) there was little to choose between the two forms of placement[7,9,12,14] while the children were placed. The main difference was that foster children had more contact with their own families. (The birth parents of adopted children often rejected them and this made decisions over adoption easier to reach.) This does not, of course, mean that there may not be differences between adopted and fostered children when the children reach adulthood. Nor does it mean that children are indifferent to whether they are adopted or not. Some children passionately want to be adopted just as others are passionately opposed to it.[12]

In practice comparison between the possible benefits of adoption and fostering is often academic. Adoption is very rarely available for foster children who are first looked after when they are over the age of six. Arguably it should be tried more often with this group and there certainly are examples of successful late adoptions.[9] However, only a small minority of foster children (in two of the York studies about one in ten) wanted to be adopted,[11,12] generally by their foster carers – sometimes as a means of 'regularising' what is in effect an adoption in all but name. Not all of these children had a foster carer who would want to adopt them. As noted above, the opposition to adoption among those who do not want it is often vehement.[12,14]

Opposition to the 'halfway house' of residence orders (or what is in some ways their successor, Special Guardianship[†]) is likely to be less vehement. Some children valued middle ways as 'more ordinary'. However, residence orders also had disad-vantages for both child and carer. The child might lose the benefits of foster care – for example, access to a local authority computer. The carer might lose financial benefits, support from the social worker and backing from the local authority if there was conflict with the birth family. Special Guardianship is, of course, as yet untested at the time of writing and the expectation is that it will attract support services. The challenge is to ensure that it avoids some of the difficulties that have faced its predecessors.

---

†   See, for example, *www.frg.org.uk/Projects/projects.asp.*

Conclusion

Since the early 1980s a change has overtaken the care system. At that time some children were looked after because of the practical difficulties of their parents; others because of their own troubles with the law or failure to attend school. These reasons are no longer enough to justify an 'admission to care'. Unaccompanied asylum-seekers may still be looked after because of their overwhelming practical difficulties. With this important exception, the care system is very heavily concentrated on children who are at risk of serious abuse or whose family relationships are dangerously fraught.

This situation may explain some of the findings of the core studies. These concentrated on children looked after at a particular point in time. They contained few of the children who leave within four weeks of entry. The 'longer-staying' children who were studied had extremely difficult backgrounds. Most did not want to go home and thought that 'being looked after' was a good idea. The likelihood of return in the near future was commonly low. Those who did return often did badly and were sometimes abused. In some cases very determined efforts had been made to keep the children at home. The consequences then were certainly a lower likelihood of adoption and probably a child who became seriously traumatised by abuse.

These problems might suggest that the children required long-term alternative families. In practice, however, very long quasi-adoptive placements were rarely on offer. In part this reflected deliberate policy. Foster care was a port in the storm, appropriate perhaps between the ages of 5 and 16, but to be avoided before and after that. Determined attempts were made to return young children to their families. At the other end of the age range, discussion when the child reached 16 years old turned to independent living; the expectation that the looked-after child moved on; and the lure of flats, freedom and leaving-care grants. In between there were the problems of breakdowns which, depending on the child's age when the placement was made, probably affected about half the children who were supposed to be placed long term.

The dilemma therefore is that at present many children can neither safely return home nor gain an alternative permanent family. This challenge is not easy to surmount. Children and families have rights. Relationships between them may be in some ways destructive. They are also strong and not to be lightly disregarded. Social workers are aware of the strength of these relationships and also of the lack of permanence in the current care system. Their managers have to contain the costs of long-term care while at the same time directing resources to acute risks within the community. For different reasons none of these groups may want an increase in the number of children supported over prolonged periods, either within the care system or outside it.

Even if these feelings and views could be ignored, the foster care system depends on exporting children to their families and independent living. If it did not do so, there would not be enough places to go round. At the minimum, therefore, the challenge is likely to require that more foster carers are recruited so that more children can stay for longer. It may also require that other children are cared for at home with a greatly increased 'package of support'.

The rest of this report is about the contribution which foster care can make to the resolution of this dilemma. It says little about work that takes place before placement and relatively little about work that takes place after it. These were not the foci of the core reports. However, there are points that can be raised. These concern:

- the comments in one report[9] that preventive work was often insufficiently intensive and prolonged but nevertheless continued at a low level to the point where the child was being seriously harmed

- the comments in another report[12] that many (not all) rehabilitated children returned to situations that were essentially unchanged and where the extent of support was far less than that available while they were in foster care.

These points raise questions about assessment, resources and systems:

- How far is it possible to make a full assessment of the situation of those who might enter foster care or who have left it? (The last York study[12] pointed out that some situations do change, albeit not always as the result of the efforts of social services departments. The joint motivation of child and parent also seemed important in ensuring success.)

- How far are the resources adequate to meet the needs raised by these assessments? (The adoption study[9] suggested that work on one problem, such as parenting skills, was not always accompanied by work on others that might be more fundamental, such as drug abuse.)

- Are these resources provided for long enough? (The adoption study[9] criticised the provision of quite intensive packages of support which were continued for a brief period of time after which the situation returned to what it had been before.)

- Are the systems of review adequate to ensure that preventive work is discontinued when it is manifestly not working? (Again, the adoption study[9] criticised work that sometimes continued for one or two years after the point when it was obvious that the situation was not going to change and that was sometimes followed by dangerous attempts at rehabilitation. Social workers, guardians and the courts could all be responsible for these unsatisfactory delays and decisions.)

In short there is a dilemma that needs to be taken seriously. Part of the solution must lie in work before and after foster care. If the numbers who are looked after are to remain at anything like the current levels, it seems essential that the support provided in the community is adequate to the level of problems the relevant children face, continued for as long as serious problems persist and accompanied by serious monitoring of the children's well-being.

The remainder of this report concentrates on another part of the solution: the role of foster care itself.

The studies suggest that the children now in the care system have left very serious situations. Some have continued in these situations to the point where they have lost any chance of adoption and their development suffers. Many of those who return home do not appear to do as well as they might have done if they had remained looked after. So it may be useful to ask:

- Is the support offered to children and their families before placement based on thorough assessment, adequate to their situation and provided for as long as there is a need for it?

- Are there adequate systems for ensuring that preventive work and attempts at rehabilitation are not continued beyond the point where they are unsafe, the child is emotionally harmed, or the child's wishes are ignored?

- Is it possible to ensure that children only return home when the situation that led to an admission has changed, both parent and child are keen 'to make a go of it', and there is an adequate support package in place?

- Where a child cannot safely return home but wishes to do so, is this dilemma acknowledged and made the focus of work so that, if possible, an acceptable compromise is reached?

Chapter 3

Developing Roles for Foster Care?

I can't tell you how lovely it was to stay in bed on Saturday morning without feeling guilty. The first two weekends I did nothing. Then I thought, this is silly. I should do something with the time. (Parent discussing a 'short break' scheme)

So he's, like, got an extra mum and dad. We get on all right. Just like a member of the extended family. (Parent describing her contact with her child's former foster carer)

Fitting in to this foster family is easy because they are my nan and grandad. (Foster child placed with relatives)

[I was unhappy] about going it alone. I didn't have any social or independence skills from my first carers. My second carers gave me a quick brush over as they did not have enough time but I needed more. (Former long-stay foster child in independent living)

Introduction

Foster care does not, for a variety of reasons, provide most children with a home for life. At the same time their family homes are often difficult places to which to return. So foster children are in danger of getting the worst of both worlds. They can return home with the attendant risks or they can be looked after in placements that do not provide a base for life.

There are three possible solutions to this dilemma. The children themselves can change so that return is easier. Alternatively, or in addition, their families can change or be better supported, perhaps in part through a different use of foster care. If neither of these things is possible, the children may need to be adopted or offered a form of foster care which is more permanent than that usually available.

This chapter discusses the implications of these 'solutions' for the kinds of foster care provided. It argues the need for:

- developing 'shared care' and 'through care'
- developing 'treatment foster care'

- developing kinship care
- enhancing long-stay foster care.

As will be seen, each of these suggestions seeks to define a role for foster care in terms of its relationship with the child's own family. Foster care may be used to supplement family care (via shared and through care), to make future family care easier (via treatment foster care) or to provide complementary families through kinship or long-stay foster care. Other roles for foster care – for example, remand fostering, short-term assessment, preparation for adoption – are obviously also required. The purpose of the chapter is therefore not to sketch out a full foster care system. Rather, in this chapter we seek to define key areas that are relevant to the dilemma outlined in the last chapter.

Shared care and through care

In this section we distinguish between 'shared care' and 'through care'. In a shared care scheme the child is placed with a carer for short breaks. The bulk of the caring continues to be done by the parents. 'Through care' is a term we use to describe the continuing involvement of the carers with a foster child after he or she has left. Through care can include an element of shared care in that children return to the carer for short breaks after they have ceased to be looked after.

One of the core studies[1] examined shared care schemes in which non-disabled pre-teenage children were placed with foster carers for an agreed series of short breaks. Parents and, in time although not necessarily at the beginning, the children greatly appreciated the voluntary and community-based nature of this service. The major difficulty related to the times when contact between carers and children ceased. These were significant events but not given much importance by the social workers involved.

Key features of these schemes included the close combination of fieldwork and placement, the continuity of carers (children returned to the same foster families) and the partnership between carer and birth parent(s). The schemes' value was enhanced by close collaboration between health visitors and social workers over referral, and by the combination of social work and other forms of support with the short breaks themselves. These features are highly relevant to more usual forms of short-stay foster care, which do not consist of an agreed series of short breaks. This type of scheme may also be relevant to long-term foster care. Many (by no means all) children in this form of care seemed to want what one young person called 'an extended family'.[12,14] These children wanted either to remain in foster care while seeing a lot of their birth family or, alternatively, to return home and see a lot of their foster carers.[11,12]

Accommodation tends to be used as a last resort rather than as a support service. In contrast, a series of short-term breaks can, if appropriately combined with other community support, offer real and valued support to parents, giving them time to get on top of their lives. The parents considering short-term breaks value time to think, an opportunity to ask questions and reassurance about their anxieties. Although children are often homesick at the start of the placement they, their parents and the carers often want the placements to continue and are sad when they end. Despite this, end-of-placement meetings are rare. Questions which arise are:

- Are short-term breaks always available to those who need this service?
- Are these breaks seen as part of a strategy to mobilise and build on community resources and are they combined with other appropriate supportive measures?
- Is the service well advertised and are the criteria for eligibility clear?
- Are parents involved in planning meetings and visiting the carer with their child before short breaks start in order to reduce the anxieties of all parties?
- Are social workers aware of the children's feelings of homesickness at the beginning, their feelings of loss at the end and the possible need for end-of-placement meetings?
- Is it possible to extend the model of support offered by short breaks to situations where the child has left foster care but is supported by his or her former carer?

The studies provide examples of such a model, albeit rarely in a fully fledged form. Relative fostering provides obvious examples.[2] There are outstanding examples of continuing shared care after a placement ending in case studies in the second York follow-up.[12] (In that study some continuing, albeit usually tapered, contact between former foster carers and adopted children was associated with good results.) More generally, many foster carers continue some, albeit usually quite limited, contact with sizeable proportions of children and young people after their departure,[12,13] or even, in some cases, placement breakdown.[14]

In general, however, the extended family concept of foster care fits ill with short-term schemes or with the general insistence that foster care is, in almost all cases, cut off when the child reaches the age of 18. It also does not fit with the lack of flexible shared care, with the care of the child variously shared between carer and birth family over a considerable time. As one report put it, 'Accommodation appears to be an all or nothing provision, rather than a negotiated, flexible service designed to meet the changing needs of the children and their families.[12]

As in the case of shared care, an extended family model of care would probably need to be combined with other forms of support. At present the families of former foster children seem to receive less support than do foster families.[12,13] They rarely, for example, have relief breaks. Parenting skills, 'vicious circles' between parent and child and school adjustment are as important at home as in foster care. Arguably the same level of support is required.

Treatment foster care

Foster care is not generally seen as a way of enabling change. This view seems to do less than justice to its potential. Foster children can test out assumptions about relationships in their new families and learn to adapt them. They have educational and other difficulties with which their carers may need to help them. US research suggests that treatment foster care can be effective, particularly if it is coherently combined with attempts to change families; for example, by training both birth families and foster families to use the same parenting approach.[23]

The research just described suggests that treatment foster care is a separate branch of foster care. In contrast, it is likely that almost *all* forms of foster care should be concerned with change. Many foster children, for example, need to develop their skills at school or come to terms with a difficult past. These are changes and foster carers are relevant to them. That said, there is also a case for some particularly well-supported and highly skilled foster care. A scheme of this kind was the focus of one of the core studies.[16]

The Scottish CAPS project studied by Walker *et al.*[16] was intended to enable change within a limited period of time. It differed from schemes currently being developed in England that build on US experience but seek to combine it with psychiatric and psychological support. The project showed at a minimum that foster care can contain some children who would otherwise be in secure provision, and that the service was appreciated, less expensive and probably more benign than secure provision. In addition the foster carers, who received excellent support, could cope. None left. These are major achievements.

Nevertheless all did not go as planned. It proved difficult to restrict the project to the children for whom it was intended. Experience also showed that the children needed longer than the six months originally planned. The time span envisaged was extended to 12 months. In addition the project was probably not suitable for all those currently sent to secure provision. Social workers certainly felt that it was difficult to do away with secure provision entirely. Some young people needed control to defuse a crisis. Some might then do well in foster care. However, some were seen as being so difficult that they could only be managed in foster care on at best a part-time basis. In addition, others might find the closeness implicit in foster care difficult or resent perceived conflict with their birth family.

It was also doubtful how far the project lived up to its remit and enabled fundamental change. Outcomes may or may not have been better than expected (there was no exact control group) but certainly showed a high level of continuing problems. Measures of 'disturbance' did not suggest that the children were fundamentally less troubled towards the end of their stay than they were at the beginning (a finding shared with other studies[3,9,11,16]). The researchers reported on 20 children who had completed their placements. Of these, six were in prison, homeless, or otherwise unsettled; nine were unemployed; and only five were in regular employment.

Three points need to be considered in relation to these difficulties. First, the placements may not have lasted long enough. Only 2 of the 20 placements completed lasted, according to social workers and carers, as long as needed. All those assessed by the researchers as getting full benefit had been there for over 18 months. The foster carers themselves highlighted the conflict between the authorities' wish to reduce placement length and their own concern for the welfare of the child.

Foster care is rarely seen as constituting a 'treatment' in its own right. American experience suggests that it could be. Experience in the CAPS project in particular shows that high-quality, well-supported placements are capable of containing some young people with very challenging behaviour without loss of foster carers. Problems in this project probably included the placing of some young people who were not suitable for it, the relatively short period of time initially allowed for the placements and the lack of attention to support after the placement ended. A number of questions arise:

- Do social workers ensure that the carers have sufficient skills and experience to take on the challenges of a given placement?
- Are there adequate risk assessments before a challenging placement is made and are adequate support packages put in place?
- Are there enough schemes of the kind provided by CAPS, particularly for adolescents?
- Do schemes such as CAPS allow sufficient time for relationships to grow between carer and foster child? Do they pay enough attention to work with the young people after the placement ends?

Many of these questions have relevance to all medium-term fostering and not simply to specialist provision.

Second, there may have been insufficient concern with what happened after the placement. The foster carers themselves were concerned about their capacity to provide 'through care'. Five local authorities funded after-care arrangements, involving contact with the carers on one or two days a week. Some carers provided respite when the young person was in residential care. Others kept informal contact, although they acknowledged new young people had to take priority and there was the problem of the distances involved.

Third, there seems to have been little attempt to ensure that the environments to which the young people returned 'fitted' their experience in foster care.

Relative foster care

Care by relatives provides a distinct way of relating foster care to the child's family. Nationally, around 16 per cent of those fostered are placed with 'relatives and friends'. Variations between authorities in the proportions of relative carers suggest that this proportion could be increased. We discuss later how this might be done. The immediate question is how far expansion is desirable.

Hunt's review of care by family and friends identifies its attractions.[4] This form of care can build on existing relationships. It often allows children to stay in the same geographical area. It should be less threatening to a child's sense of belonging to a family, build on and strengthen a family's ability to offer care, reduce the child's trauma of moving to an unknown family and, perhaps, make it easier to keep siblings together. Hunt's review provides evidence for many of these potential advantages. She adds evidence that children see relative placements more positively than stranger placements, that carer and child may be closer in such placements, and that the placements themselves tend to last longer.

Additional advantages for continuing or shared care by a relative are that it does not deprive other potential foster children of foster care and it may also make it easier for children to remain in the same area when they cease to be looked after.[4] There is a further potential advantage that seems to be exploited less than it might. Ethnic matching is sometimes difficult, particularly in areas where there are, for example, few people from a child's ethnic group. Relative fostering has the potential to overcome this problem. For these reasons relative care may be a good way of offering both shared care and extended care.

In the other core studies only the York research considered care by relatives at any length. Relative foster care was under-represented in this research and the number of kin carers involved was small (25 relative carers in the study of foster children and 70 in the study of carers). The results suggested that outcomes were neither better nor worse for kinship care. (This result is in keeping with Hunt's review[4] where some outcome studies found better results and others worse ones.)

These apparently equivalent results were achieved with seemingly lower levels of support and in contexts of some difficulty.[10] In comparison with other carers, relatives tended to be poorer, less highly educated and less well remunerated by social services. They also received less training and less support from supervising social workers. Family disputes were very common – in fact almost universal – in this group. These either pre-existed the placement or arose in relation to it – for example, when aunts disputed with each other over who should take a child or a parent wished to visit the placement with her boyfriend against the wishes of social services.

These results are in keeping with Hunt's review.[4] They show that relative care has difficulties as well as advantages. In keeping with this Triseliotis *et al.*[15] report professional concern about the growing use of relative placements in Scotland. This focuses on relatives' limited resources; their inability, sometimes, to protect children from abuse within the family; the criminal records of some of them; and often their reluctance to work with social workers. In the adoptions study[9] a number of children were placed with relatives before final plans were made.

> Seventy per cent of [these] placements disrupted. Kin placements disrupted for three main reasons. First, relatives did not protect the child because they did not believe the allegations and allowed unrestricted contact. Second, the birth parent was so violent that relatives became afraid for their own and the child's safety. Finally the relatives often had unrealistic expectations and could not cope with the child's needs or behaviour.

These studies rightly warn that kinship care has its own problems. They do not necessarily imply that there should not be more of it. An alternative response could be, for example, to provide these carers with more support. More recently Farmer and Moyers have carried out a much bigger study of kinship care[17] than those discussed so far. They compared 142 children placed with relatives and friends with 128 children placed with unrelated foster carers. The first group were predominantly with grandparents (46%) or aunts and uncles (32%). In many respects the children in kinship care were very similar to those fostered with others. The two groups were of similar ages, exhibited similar behaviour before placement and had a similar frequency of adversities in their backgrounds.

In terms of differences, children placed with relatives or friends were less likely to have a parent who had been in care, or to have suffered 'emotional difficulties' before placement. Their carers were more likely to be in financial difficulty. (Financial problems were probably not eased by the transfer of some carers to less financially rewarded residence orders.) Relative/friend carers were also more likely to have a chronic illness or disability, live in overcrowded conditions, be receiving very little social work support and be ethnically matched with the child. (In sharp contrast to US research, children from an ethnic minority were less likely to be placed with kin than other children.) As the literature would predict, children fostered by relatives and friends were closer to the parental home, and had much higher levels of contact with other members of their family (a result also found in York study 2[11]).

The researchers were less likely to rate the children's contact with families as detrimental. They also found less tension between foster and other children in the same house than in unrelated households. In contrast, as in York study 2,[11] they were much more likely to note disputes between carers and family members (in 54% as against 16% of cases). They also felt that relative carers were much more likely to be struggling to cope with the children they looked after (45% vs 30%) and were more likely to have poor parenting skills (25% vs 12%). By way of compensation the carers were much more likely to be highly committed to the child (63% vs 31%). In keeping with this the placements were almost invariably initiated at the suggestion of the relative or the child. They were rarely sought out by the social workers.

In general the researchers' measures of outcome and their overall judgements of the effects of the placements showed very little difference between the two types of placement. As in York study 2,[11] placements with carers related to them were no more or less likely to break down. They were, however, more likely to *last*. This almost certainly reflected the fact that they were intended to last – plans for relative placements were much more likely to be for a long stay. (In this respect relative placements may sometimes act as an alternative to adoption. York study 2[11] contained a small number of long-lasting placements for young children who were of an age to be adopted but who were nevertheless fostered with relatives or on residence orders with them.)

So, relative placements have much to recommend them. They are not, however, a free lunch. Their advantages are likely to stem in part from their 'naturalness' and the commitment of those involved. In most cases the commitment overcomes the disadvantages that flow from poverty and, perhaps, a lower degree of parenting skill than that found among 'ordinary foster carers'. Better financial and social work support and more appropriate training might further lessen these disadvantages. In contrast, attempts to extend the quantity of relative care in the unreflective belief that relative care is 'better' might result in the recruitment of some 'reluctant relatives': the present group largely volunteer themselves. This in turn might lower placement quality. Less committed carers might be recruited. In other cases contact with a relative might be detrimental and this contact might be hard to avoid.

The challenge to practitioners is thus to develop care by relatives and friends, keeping its advantages and reducing its difficulties.

Placements with relatives have numerous potential advantages. They draw on commitment and family loyalty. They usually keep the child in familiar surroundings. They are not liable to be cut off at the age of 18. They may make ethnic matching easier. They do not reduce the number of vacancies in 'ordinary fostering'. However, relative carers tend to be poorer and worse housed than others. They may be in dispute with the child's family or find it difficult to protect the child from undesirable contacts. Questions which arise include:

- Are relative placements routinely considered when a child is fostered?
- Are there policies to promote their availability?
- Is there an awareness of both their potential advantages and potential disadvantages?
- Are steps taken to promote the advantages and reduce the difficulties?

Long-stay foster care

Some children cannot return home and therefore require some form of long-stay substitute care. The core studies examine a variety of forms of this care – adoption by strangers, adoption by carers, residence orders with carers, residence orders with relatives, and long-stay foster care itself.

Comparison between these different forms of care was unusual. Only three studies[9,12,14] were able to compare sizeable numbers of adopted children with sizeable numbers of children in long-term foster care. Only one[12] compared residence orders with foster care. Such comparisons are difficult since it is very hard to make sure that like is being compared with like. In general the comparisons suggest:

- While the children were being brought up there seemed very little to distinguish the outcomes of long-stay foster care and adoption.[9,12,14] Where differences were found they seemed to favour adoption[8,12] and to relate in particular to the nature or strength of attachments.[9,12]

- Long-term foster carers often felt hampered in acting as parents (e.g. in taking responsibility over education) by the lack of a clear division of responsibility between themselves and social workers.[9] They also complained of the expectation that young people start to move on between the ages of 16 and 18, seeing this practice as unsettling and unfair to the young people.

- Children themselves, once they were of an age to express an opinion, had very strong views on whether they wished to be adopted or fostered.[12,14] Only a minority (about 10%) wanted to be adopted, almost always by their carers. As described in Chapter 2, the chance of adoption reduced sharply as the age of the child increased and was thus affected by prolonged and unsuccessful attempts at prevention or rehabilitation.

- Carer adoptions were, if anything, even more successful than stranger ones at the start of placement, but their frequency was reduced by reluctance on the part of some professionals to sanction them[9,12] (see also Lowe *et al.*[20] and Ward *et al.*[22]) and by the reluctance of carers to lose financial and other supports (Kirton *et al.*[5]). Moreover, their apparent advantages at the beginning[9,12] may have become less apparent over time.[9]

In practice adoption was not a possibility for most children. The reason was partly age – children who were first fostered when aged six or over were hardly ever adopted – and partly the unwillingness of most older children to be adopted. Carers who might consider adopting (and nearly four in ten do at some point[5]) were not always matched with children who wished to be adopted, and were sometimes dissuaded by fears of losing necessary finance or support.[5,12] The frequency of residence orders was similarly reduced by carer concerns. They valued the greater freedom from local authority involvement but feared the loss of financial and other forms of support.

Children who cannot return home may want to be adopted, fostered or provided with some other form of long-term care. Possibilities, other than long-term fostering, are sometimes reduced by a lack of decisiveness and a reluctance to sanction carer adoptions or provide them with adequate support. Long-term foster care itself is very rarely 'a base for life'. Questions which arise include:

- Are attempts to return young children to their homes or keep them there continued beyond the point where they have any reasonable chance of success and without the formulation of alternative plans in case of failure?

- Are carer adoptions, residence orders or the use of Special Guardianship discouraged by official disapproval, or the loss of necessary financial or moral support?

- Are long-term carers clear about their roles in relation to education?

- How far are long-term foster care placements explicitly seen as permanent?

- How easy is it for young people to stay with their carers beyond the age of 18 if both carer and children want this?

- Are adoptive parents able to access a similar quality of support to that available to foster carers?

Conclusion

Foster children vary in the way they see the relationship between their foster families and their home. The suggestions in this chapter are intended to allow for these varied perceptions. Taken together they would help to build a system of foster care in which:

- there is more choice of provision
- the relationships between carers and children are valued and, if appropriate, continued after the children have left
- foster care itself is seen as a potential source of change
- there is more coherence between what happens in foster care and what happens after it
- the potential contribution of relative carers is appreciated and given greater support while not being automatically endorsed.

The suggestions blur the differences between these various forms of provision. Adoption with contact and support is no longer so sharply different from fostering. Nor is fostering which continues to provide support after 18 so clearly marked out from adoption. Special Guardianship may be a better choice in some cases than either adoption or foster care. Equally it might be seen as an unsatisfactory compromise or as an unnecessary formalisation of a long-term arrangement that is working well. Shared care might merge into 'extended family care' or vice versa, and either might need to incorporate elements of 'treatment foster care'. Similarly children and carers sometimes choose each other and the label (adoption, fostering, or other) under which they wish to conduct their relationship. It is important that social services are in a position not to have to stand in their way.

Some foster children want to go home and can safely do so. Others are not so lucky. Foster care has to be sufficiently varied to allow for these different situations and for intermediate ones where, for example, children can return with intensive support. Against this background the core studies highlight the potential of shared care, care by relatives, intensive fostering schemes targeted at difficult adolescents, and more permanent foster care. Questions which arise include:

- Should there be more shared or extended care in which care is genuinely shared between carers and parents either instead of 'ordinary' foster care or after it?

- Should there be more treatment foster care in which foster care itself is seen as an important agent for change and not just a setting in which others deliver treatment?

- Should there be changes in long-stay foster care so that it becomes a genuine alternative to adoption, in the sense of offering extended care in one family with support from that family after the child has reached the age of 18?

- Are the advantages and potential difficulties of relative care appreciated and is appropriate support for relative carers provided?

- What is the role and potential of Special Guardianship?

Chapter 4

What Should Foster Care Provide?

My mum goes, 'Don't call them…[Mum and Dad] because they're not.' Then [my sister] told me to call them Mummy and Daddy Potter when my mum wasn't around, so I called them that when my mum wasn't around, and then when my mum was there, it was Linda and Nigel. (Foster child)

Some people say, 'Yeah, but that sort of thing goes on in all families' and I'm like, 'Well, how am I supposed to know that?' I mean I've been in care ten years, and it's just not like not a normal family do you know what I mean…it's foster mum and dad and foster kids. It's not normal at all. (Foster child)

I love where I am because they are like my real family. I love them with all my heart. (Foster child)

[Foster care] is lots of moving about – different sets of rules, never knew where I stood…no control over my life – everyone making decisions without me. (Foster child)

If it had not been for my foster carers I would not have passed my GCSEs, went to college and achieved a GNVQ in social care… [I wouldn't have been interested] in work at a nursing home or doing a college course. (Foster child)

Introduction

Foster care is both like and unlike family care. Families are expected to provide certain things: love, for example, and moral training. What should foster care provide? This is partly a question of children's rights:[16] an issue of morality, law and European and United Nations Conventions. It also depends on 'matters of fact': what the children want, what they need and what outcomes it is possible to achieve for them.

This chapter examines these 'matters of fact'. The description of 'wants' is largely concerned with the immediate features of foster care – for example, with the degree to which the children wanted it to be 'more normal'. The discussion of 'needs' is more concerned with the child's whole career in the care system and out of it. Different kinds of foster care may provide for these needs to differing extents; in general, the longer foster care lasts the more central it is likely to be in meeting a child's needs. Nevertheless it matters less who meets the child's needs than that somebody does.

What did the children want?

Foster children differ in ages, gender and ethnicity. They have differing histories, personalities and abilities. Unsurprisingly, different foster children want different things. Despite these differences all foster children face some common issues. They are not living with their families. They are in somebody else's house and are expected to abide by their rules. Their future is not secure: they can be moved against their wishes and their expectations. Their lives are encompassed with regulations. Their friends are unlikely to see their situation as 'normal'.

Against this background the studies suggest that children have five main requirements:

1. *Normality.* Children want fostering to be as 'normal' as possible. They do not like having to delay decisions about going on school trips or 'sleep-overs' to be put off while permission is sought from a social worker. They do not like to be embarrassed at school because reviews are held there about them or because their method of getting to school (e.g. by taxi) singles them out.[9,11,12,13]

2. *Family care.* Children want to feel that they belong in their foster home, that they are treated the same as other children in their home and, ideally, that they are loved, listened to and encouraged. They resent harsh or inconsistent discipline, and any feeling that their foster carers are 'just doing it for the money'. They value treats, opportunities for their hobbies and, in most cases, a room of their own.[11,12,13] (See also Harwin *et al.*[19] and Packman and Hall.[21])

3. *Respect for their origins.* Children do not want a conflict of loyalty between their foster carer and their family. As discussed earlier they have differing views about how far they want to belong to their own family or to their foster family and about which members of their family they wish to see. They want these views respected.[2,11,12]

4. *Control.* Foster children want serious attention paid to their views. They differ in their requirements for a placement. Some want to be with other children, some like houses in which there are babies, some want to be with their siblings, and so on. They differ in how happy they are in their placements, in the relationship they would like to see between their placement and home, in the members of their family they want to see, in the frequency with which they want to see social workers and in much else besides. They do not like situations in which it is not clear what plans there are for them or in which they are moved suddenly and with little notice. They want social workers to be aware of their feelings on these matters and to take action accordingly.[11,12,13]

5.   *Opportunity.* There is no evidence that foster children differ from others in what they want for their futures. Success at school, a good job, a happy family and children are all common aspirations. It is arguable that, like many of us, they want the result but not the means necessary to get it. Success at school may be more desired than homework. There is some evidence that their aspirations are limited.[13] Nevertheless, the safest assumption is that they want foster care to be a springboard for getting their lives in order and on track for what most would regard as success.[11,12,13,16] Carers were praised not only for providing a family environment and making the children feel valued but also for offering opportunities and enabling skills.[13]

What did the children need?

Judgements of need depend on views of what is 'a good life' for foster children and on theories of what they require to achieve it. The core studies use a variety of these theories. One study[7] refers to attachment theory, theories of the consequence of maltreatment, and theories relating to the issues in adoption and the proper way to parent. Another[16] refers to attachment theory, 'cognitive task' models, resilience theory and ideas about the opportunities and risks posed by a 'less rigidly structured society'.

In selecting these theories the researchers could point to the children's characteristics and their apparent consequences. As has been seen the children commonly have histories of defective parenting, maltreatment, confused or poor attachments and frequent separations. Research suggests maltreatment makes it difficult for children to regulate their emotions. It also leads to poor or confused attachments, poor peer relationships and a poorly developed 'self-system'. It seems natural to think that their road to a better future lies in counteracting the effects of abuse and making good the difficulties in attachment.

Abuse is linked to another key feature, poor school performance.[7] One study[12] found that a simple variable, unhappiness at school, predicted a wide variety of problems three years later. In addition lack of qualifications may make it difficult for foster children to make their way in a world where possible future roles are less clearly laid out and much depends on a person's skills. Schooling is another key target for intervention.

'Resilience theory' is probably the most general of the theories used. Essentially it is a list of 'protective factors' thought to increase the chance of good outcomes among children otherwise at risk of poor ones. Different writers produce different lists of these factors. Most lists include the presence of a good attachment, the opportunity to make a new start and a good educational experience. These seem achievable goals for foster care. They are relevant to the children's difficulties. They are in line with what the children want.

These requirements suggest other less general theories that are relevant to foster care. Successful parents provide opportunities for attachment and encouragement to do well at school. So theories of parenting are relevant to the tasks foster carers undertake. These theories generally emphasise the need for parents to combine support with control or guidance.[7] In line with this, social workers look to placements to provide adolescents with stability, nurture and clear guidance. Older foster children want to be valued by their carers and dislike approaches to discipline that they perceive as harsh, unreasonable or unfair. Foster parents may need to be particularly skilled if they are to provide appropriate discipline without making their foster children feel rejected.[6]

Similarly, foster children may only be able to make a new start and move on if they can make sense of their situation. They have to come to terms with their relationship with their birth family, their anomalous situation in someone else's family and perhaps their ethnicity. Theories of identity are relevant to these tasks. The studies provide plenty of evidence that foster children are concerned with these issues. They resent attempts to interfere with their view of their family relationships. They value carers who support their view of their own ethnicity. They may also value a chance to talk these things over. Many want no more than a sympathetic, impartial ear.

This general framework is consistent with the expectations with which children were placed in the CAPS study.[16] Those outside the placements expected them to provide stability and nurture within the family (partly to prepare for returning to a family or founding families of their own), consistent boundaries for behaviour, encouragement of school or work, reparation of past trauma, a chance to renew or develop relationships with parents or relatives, and a chance to prepare for independent living (e.g. learning to use services, shop, buses etc.). Carers were also expected to have concerns for health (notably through the child's GP). This list of requirements was developed for a specialised scheme but could arguably apply much more widely.

A reasonably comprehensive list of the key needs of foster children would therefore include:

- 'good enough' parenting (nurture and 'boundaries'), probably informed by additional insights from social learning and attachment theory
- the development or support of good attachments
- good education and experiences of school
- support for the children in developing their sense of identity – particularly as this refers to their relationship with their family, their experience as a foster child, their ethnicity[14] and their general view of themselves
- support for friendships and the development of skills and interests.[3]

This list of needs would probably be accepted by most of the researchers involved in the core studies. It provides reasonable pointers to the principles and practice that need to underpin foster care.

In the following sections we discuss four key principles. These focus on four 'Cs': close relationships, change and development, choice and coherence. They are justified by combining what most foster children appear to want with what most probably need.

Close relationships

Children wanted relationships and they needed them. More specifically, they wanted to see more of their families or particular members of them. They valued the love and concern of their foster carers. They sometimes looked back with sadness on the loss of particular social workers or foster carers who had been very important to them. Some complained that their carers looked after them for reasons of money not love. Those who were said to have a strong relationship with a particular adult had better outcomes.[12]

Foster carers also valued relationships. They pointed to the key importance of commitment to the children. They often timed their departure from fostering to coincide with the departure of the foster children.[7] Relationships were the basis of this commitment and of their satisfaction. Placements broke down because of a breakdown in relationships.[11] Care leavers did better if they had a close relationship with at least one adult.[12]

In these ways relationships were at once the basis for placements, the enabler of longer-term careers and a potential focus for work. Our first principle is that the practice of foster care should enable and value the children's positive relationships, whether these are with members of their family or extended family, foster carers, counsellors, teachers or anyone else. Social workers and foster carers should be aware of the positive relationships that children have and make it their business to nurture them.

Most people will find this principle obvious. It is, however, worth stressing since it is not always followed. An emphasis on relationship sits uneasily with a system in which foster children effectively have to leave at the age of 18 and in which the pain of partings – commonly felt by carers, carers' children and foster children themselves – may not even be acknowledged.[1] It may also be perceived as in conflict with an emphasis on foster care as a professional and increasingly expensive resource.

Change and development

The children wanted successful futures. We have argued that they needed parenting which was able to guide as well as nurture and also a good experience of school. Some want, and arguably need, an opportunity to talk through issues about their identity – for example, what it means to be a child of a particular ethnicity, or one who comes from a particular family, or one who is a foster child. The practice of fostering therefore needs to emphasise the acquisition of skills, good schooling and the sense in the children that they can be happy with themselves and also successful people.

These requirements may be met in various ways (e.g. at home or in foster care). They may also seem obvious. Again, however, the practice of fostering does not always emphasise them. For example, residential care may be seen as therapeutic and 'enabling change'. Children change in foster care but this is hardly ever the explicit aim of the placement.[11] Treatment takes place within the context of foster care, not as part of it. Even in this limited form, treatment of any intensity is not always available. Paradoxically, the most damaged children in the core studies attracted very large sums of money but almost nothing in terms of either comprehensive assessment or intensive therapeutic intervention.[9]

Choice

Unsurprisingly, foster children want to be heard and to get more of what they want. This desire relates to their contacts with their family, the particular kind of foster family they want, the way decisions are taken in their normal lives (normality), their long-term future (whether to go home) and much else besides. The children have a right to be heard on these issues. There is also evidence that foster children who want to be fostered are less likely to have placement breakdowns as, probably, are those who have 'chosen' their foster carers.[23]

Clearly children cannot have everything they want. It is, however, possible and desirable to seek to know what they want and for policy makers to take these 'wants' into account. This principle is again widely accepted. However, as will be seen later, it is easily breached. For example, social workers may not know that a child wants to see a particular member of his or her extended family.[3] Equally, many fewer children stay on with their foster carers after they reach the age of 18 than arguably wish to do so.[11,12]

Coherence

Our fourth principle of 'coherence' cuts across the others. It concerns the relationship between what happens in foster care and what happens after it. As we have seen, the key potential weakness of the foster care system is, perhaps, not so much what goes on in the system itself but later events. Relatively long-stay foster children going home often seemed to do 'worse' than would have been the case if they had stayed with their carers. Nevertheless, they commonly go home, sometimes because they, their parents or the courts insist on it, and sometimes because social workers have run out of other options. Such returns are necessary for the system. If they did not occur there would not be enough foster carers to go round. If returns are not to be detrimental the child or the family or both have to change or very high levels of support have to be given.

In our view there is a danger of 'incoherence' if:

- relationships between the child and others are arbitrarily cut off (as discussed above)

- a child remains in foster care for a while and then returns home when there is no evidence that anything essential has changed

- there is a lack of fit between what the child 'learns' in foster care and what happens when he or she leaves (e.g. child acquires A levels but has no back-up for making use of them)

- there is discontinuity of support – for example, the child and foster family receive intensive support while the child is fostered but subsequently there is nothing comparable for the birth family.

Again this principle may seem obvious. It is, however, quite regularly breached. Foster children are expected to perform at school as a way into jobs but then routinely enter low-level jobs for which only minimal education is necessary.[12] Support for families, low enough while the children are in foster care, is routinely very low indeed once they leave it and return home.[12]

Conclusion

Social services are concerned with what children want. Undoubtedly they seek to ensure that this concern is exemplified in foster placements and what goes before and after them. They may nevertheless find that:

- Procedure and practice unintentionally mark the children out as different from their peers. Foster carers may feel unable to authorise sleep-overs and school trips or other day-to-day matters that are normally managed by parents. Children may not be encouraged to tell their social workers about any practice about which they are uneasy, including the venue for meetings, methods of transport to school, their uniform and the information available to teachers about them. Distinguishing marks that cannot be avoided (for example, differences in name between carer and child) may not be discussed.

- Children's requirements for family care, respect for their origins, control and opportunity are not routinely met. Carers are likely to be aware of them. Many, for example, go to great lengths to ensure that the foster children are treated as part of the family. Nevertheless these requirements are not easy to meet. It is, for example, very difficult to make someone feel at home in one's house. Moreover these issues are not necessarily stressed in the training of social workers and foster carers or reinforced through the use of experienced carers and foster children or through regular discussion between social workers and foster carers.

- Foster children may find it difficult to make their wishes known. They are only likely to get what they want if social workers and foster carers know what this is. This partly depends on the foster children themselves. Those who are old enough might perhaps be provided with courses on 'how to get the most out of foster care'. However, it also depends on the ability of foster carers to listen creatively and the skill of social workers at interviewing children of different ages. It may also depend on formal provisions (e.g. on ensuring that each long-stay foster child has a 'champion').

- Foster children may have inaccurate ideas of their situation. They are only likely to feel they have some control over their situation if they are aware of the plans that have been made for them and if these plans are kept up to date. Social services obviously try to be meticulous in ensuring that foster children are kept up to date in this way and that the information is provided in a way that the children can take in. As will be seen later, these efforts are not always successful.

- There may be a greater willingness to spend money on confronting problems than on enabling foster children to use opportunities which school or foster care offers and which may develop their abilities.

The evidence on what children need has very wide implications. It underpins much in the report. For the moment we would argue that all foster carers and social workers should have an understanding of:

- the key factors associated with resilience
- attachment theory and its broad implications for foster care
- the importance of schooling for foster care
- the key qualities of parents and their implications for foster care
- the relevance of social learning theory for the guidance and control of older children.

It might be argued that foster carers and social workers are already well aware of attachment theory. However, the pressures of work may make this knowledge hard to apply. Similarly it may be believed that professionalism implies an emotional detachment from the children rather than an ability to think dispassionately without losing commitment. Similar criticisms might be made of the foster care system in general. At one level foster families operate like ordinary ones on the basis of relationships. When foster children leave, the system operates as if the families had been hotels or hospitals – places where children were parked and lodged and whose custodians must now move on to other duties. Foster carers and children commonly do keep in touch, but this is something that happens 'unofficially'. In this way the foster care system may be in danger of squandering its greatest asset, what one study describes as the 'emotional capital' it builds up.[11]

Longer-staying foster children want normality, a family which accepts them, respect for their origins, an important voice in decisions about them and a springboard to a better life. Most probably need an experience of 'good enough parenting', support for developing or maintaining attachments, encouragement to enjoy school and do well there, and support for developing a sense of identity. A system designed to meet both wishes and needs would, in our view, be based on principles relating to close relationships, change, choice and coherence.

- How far are policies and practices in foster care, along with the training of carers and social workers, routinely informed by a coherent understanding of what children want and need?
- How far are they informed by a desire to promote close relationships, change and choice?
- How far is foster care consciously designed so that it is coherent with practice before and after it?

Chapter 5

Placing Children in Foster Care

[Being placed was] rushed and I was not given a choice because social services had nowhere to put me. (Foster child)

I do worry about Mrs Wright. Her house is so nice, fresh, you know. Tracy is old enough to see the difference. I worry it might turn her against me, make her realise what we don't have. (Parent of foster child)

[Being placed was] upsetting because I didn't know anyone but I came with my sister so I felt OK. (Foster Child)

Introduction

This chapter is the first to consider what makes placements work. It examines the making of placements: the point at which the foundations for the placement are laid. These foundations may, or may not, be in keeping with the principles outlined in the last chapter. For example, previous close relationships may be maintained or start to wither. There may or may not be a viable educational plan. Children may feel that they have a say in what occurs or feel powerless. They may or may not feel that they have been able to maintain valued links with their previous lives. The purpose of this chapter is to illustrate these processes, identify variables that may influence their course and examine their apparent effects on outcomes.

We consider:

- how placements were made
- how the different parties felt about the process
- whether they felt consulted and involved
- whether the process of making placements influenced outcomes.

How are placements made?

The process of making a placement is embedded in a wider process of care planning.[19,20,21] Possible participants in this process include social workers, their managers, legal departments, parents, children, 'guardians' and the courts. These parties have different interests, do not necessarily agree and have varying degrees of experience of the system. The criteria against which decisions are made are loose and rarely written down. Plans change in response to shortages of resources and the actions of individuals. The meetings at which plans are 'firmed up' are not easy for children and parents and may be experienced as accusatory. Many decisions are made at short notice, as a matter of emergency and in a highly charged atmosphere.

In such a situation there is much scope for misunderstanding and much difficulty in enabling children and their parents to express informed preferences on clear-cut options. The core studies were concerned less with these wider processes than with the making of individual placements. Here there were differences between placements for long-term or specialised foster care, and those for 'ordinary foster care'. The latter included both emergency and short-term placements and longer-term placements that did not go through a panel. Placements for the shared care scheme[1] were, to some extent, a special case.

The studies of special schemes or long-term placements[7,8,14,16] suggested a process that moved quite deliberately. Standard forms were completed, panels considered the decisions involved, carers were invited to consider whether they were suitable and so on. Many of these placements were in fact for adoption. (Findings on adoptive placements are included here, partly for their intrinsic interest. Moreover, arrangements for making foster care placements that duplicate those for adoption are likely to produce similar difficulties.) The decisions involved were often inherently difficult. For example, there were conflicts between the need to achieve 'permanence' (which might suggest that children should stay with those with whom they had bonded) and a good match on grounds of ethnicity, placement with siblings and so on[8,14] (see also Ward *et al.*[22]). There were also problems over a lack of resources.

All this could result in:

- *varying amounts of social work preparation of the child* – in the sibling study six out of ten received substantial work from social workers but some received little or none[8]

- *lack of adequate assessments of particular aspects of relationships between siblings* – these were not always assessed even when workers disagreed on whether siblings should be placed together[8]

- *little use of standard tests of psychological state* – these were rarely available[13]

- *difficulties in creating an adequate educational plan* – these were particularly pronounced when the placing authority differed from the authority in which the child was placed.[16]

Placements in 'ordinary foster care' suggested even more severe difficulties. Here the process was marked by:

- lack of choice – choice of placement was probably available in only around 30 per cent of cases[3,11]

- a feeling of crisis with social workers commonly describing the placements as emergencies[3,11]

- a need to accept that some initial placements would not be fully satisfactory[11]

- a willingness to wait for suitable long-term placements – a process which resulted in a high proportion which were seen as suitable, but also in lengthy stays in initial placements which were not necessarily prepared for this.[11]

What do the children feel about the process?

For the children the process of placement is fraught. Commonly it follows a very difficult time for them. They may worry about the meaning of the event. How far is it their fault? Did they cause a previous placement to break down? Is their family rejecting them? Why are they placed and not their siblings? How long will the placement last? Will those at home get along without them?[23]

At the same time they are going to a new family with unfamiliar rules and customs. They may not know whether people in this household flush the lavatory in the night, they may miss their favourite television programme, they may be given food they particularly do not like. They may miss their family, pets or school friends. Asked for suggestions some emphasised the need for children to be given a chance to see if they would fit in to a new family before committing themselves.[3,11] At the least they wanted a full picture of the new family before they moved.[3]

These problems even occurred in the short-stay placements.[1] Children in the shared care scheme were anxious about going away, homesick and worried that they might lose their family altogether. They were aware of the potential stigma of help from social services and reluctant to raise their experiences at school. They were most likely to talk to their parents about this (a resource not so easily available to children in long-term placements) or to their carers. Some of them talked to no one and they rarely confided in social workers, teachers and friends. Many managed their sadness by going to their rooms to be alone. Such problems are likely to be even more severe in long-stay placements.

What do parents feel about the process?

The birth parents of placed children are also unlikely to find the experience an easy one. Some indeed may feel a sense of relief. They may have been at the end of their tether with a young baby, found it impossible to manage a teenager or even been frightened of their own children. They may have actually been battling with social services to notice their plight. Even in these cases, however, there are likely to be mixed emotions, feelings of loss, a sense of failure, a worry about how the event can be presented at school or to the neighbours, a concern about how their child may do when away from them and about whether he or she will cease to love them or fail to return.[23]

Such feelings are likely to be stronger when the removal is compulsory and involves imputations of fault. Nevertheless, they were found to apply even when children were only placed for weekends with short-term carers. Parents in the short-term study[1] were very pleased with their short-term breaks, but still they worried that they would lose their children, that they would be stigmatised as poor parents, or that their children would turn against them.

What do carers feel about the process?

The carers or adopters in these cases also experienced difficulties. In the case of adopters these seemed to stem from an unequal balance of power between the adopter, who wanted a child, and the social worker, who was seen as able to withhold one. Foster carers, in contrast, felt pressured to take children who otherwise might not be placed at all. The problems included:

- pressure to include 'higher risk' cases than the carers thought appropriate for their special scheme[16] or to agree to conditions such as family contact which adopters thought inappropriate[12]

- parental assessments which were perceived as threatening by adopters, who did not object to the need for assessment but did sometimes object to the feeling that the criteria against which they were assessed were unclear and informed by judgements about such things as Christian belief[12]

- delays in making placements, some of which were perceived by adoptive parents as relating to administrative inefficiency, and which were not always accompanied by information on the reasons for and likely length of the delay[12]

- a feeling among some adoptive parents that they had been given too rosy or too poor a picture of the child.[12] In one study[9] 58 per cent of the carers and 68 per cent of the adoptive parents felt that they had not been given adequate information. Other studies[3,12] similarly emphasised the high proportion of carers who felt that they did not have enough information.

Do carers, children and parents feel consulted?

These processes could lead to a lack of partnership between carer, child, birth family and social workers. Carers in particular complained of lack of adequate information, lack of clarity over plans and in some cases 'arm-twisting' to take cases for which they felt their family was not suitable. In other research four out of ten carers who were looking after a sexually abused child had not been told of the abuse.[18] As there was evidence that half the sexually abused children abused others during their time of being looked after, this was clearly information in which carers had an interest.

The study of teenage fostering[3] provided a clear example of these processes. In that study just over a quarter of the foster carers said that they felt under at least some pressure to take the child. In two thirds of all the cases the social workers and carers had a different understanding of the plan (in 22% of cases there were no plans). Four out of ten carers complained they did not get the information they needed and just over a quarter said the information was inaccurate. As for the young people, 82 per cent of the foster children either felt not involved at all (30%) or only briefly (52%). A fifth had met the foster carers before but around three quarters had little or no contact before moving in. There was said to be discussion with parents in only 37 per cent of cases. In only 31 per cent of cases was there discussion with everyone.

The fullest discussion of the involvement of parents comes from the contact study.[2] In that study parents' attitude to the process of placement depended on whether they wanted the placement at all. Those who did not want the child placed typically did not approve of the process of making the placement. Generally the parents seem to have felt quite powerless. They did not feel they had control over the decision to accommodate the child, or the choice of foster carers (which they did not expect), and in only a third of cases were they involved in decisions about contact. Commonly they felt distress on being parted from their children and had few resources to cope with this.

The study provided information on pre-placement meetings. A quarter of the children already knew their carers. Where they did not, pre-placement meetings took place in only half the cases. The parents (or at least the mothers, for social workers rarely worked with fathers) welcomed these, although some felt ill prepared, inadequate or excluded, or that decisions had been made prior to the meeting. If they did not know the foster carers, they rarely met them in advance, although most would have liked to do this. They rarely talked to the children about the forthcoming move and rarely accompanied them to see the foster carer.

In this study social workers were better at assessing the views of older children. A quarter of the younger children did not know how long they would be fostered. Generally, there was a considerable disparity in the reasons why children thought they were fostered, why parents thought this, and why the social worker thought this. A quarter of the children in the intensive study had no idea. As in the adolescent fostering study,[3] and indeed in York study 2,[11] foster carers commonly had different ideas to those of the social worker as to the purpose and likely duration of the placement.

The most positive experience of consultation was probably reported in the study of short-term placements.[1] Here health visitors helped to reassure parents that the short-term placements were normal and likely to be helpful. Social workers spent much time reassuring parents that the provision was intended to help them and not a response to failure. Parents generally appreciated these attempts to involve and consult them, although their understanding of their problems did not always appear to match that of the social workers and some preferred to be quiet in meetings. For their part the children seemed to feel that they were much less involved and consulted than the social workers implied. The researchers considered that in many cases the children had little choice over whether they were to remain with their families at all. They suggested it was poor practice to pretend that a choice existed when it did not.

Does the way placements were made influence outcomes?

How far did 'good' or 'bad' experiences of placement influence subsequent events? Previous research suggested that placements made 'in a rush' were more likely to fail. The study of teenage placements[3] provided similar evidence:

- Emergency placements for young people were more likely to disrupt, usually for reasons connected with behaviour.

- Young people who felt fully involved in the placement decision, those who had foster carers who were involved in discussions and those who had prior contact with carers were more (but not significantly more) likely to be there on follow-up.

- Young people whose carers said they had been given inadequate information about their school attendance and about the long-term plan for education/employment were more likely to have disrupted placements as were those where carers said they did not have information on how long the child was to stay.

- Young people whose carers found them no more difficult to manage than they expected had fewer disrupted placements. (Arguably, they displayed no difficult behaviour but it may also be that carers who had been prepared were more willing to tolerate difficulties.)

- Young people who were not of the gender for which carers expressed a preference were more likely to have disrupted placements.

- Young people who felt they had been consulted were rated as having more successful placements, as were those who found the placement better than they expected.

- Young people who had been given placements which were not thought fully satisfactory for them at the time were more likely to fail – at least over the first year of the placement.[11] Such placements were much more likely where there had been no choice of placement: a situation more likely when the placement was 'an emergency'.

Three of the studies[8,9,12] pointed particularly to the importance of previous foster carers in smoothing transitions to new long-term (usually adoptive) placements. Usually, but not always, this went well. In satisfactory handovers the previous carer was careful to welcome the new ones, to encourage the child to view the new placement positively (e.g. by praising their new bedroom if they saw it) and providing the new carers with key information on the child's behaviour, likes and dislikes over food and so on. One study suggested that the new placements went better if the former carer did not simply disappear but instead had some contact with the child which gradually tapered off. Failure to do this was felt by some parents to leave the child feeling rejected and, perhaps, to leave the child believing that the move to the new placement had been made because he or she had been 'naughty'.[12]

It is difficult to be sure as to whether an unsatisfactory placement process 'causes' poor outcomes. Young people who have emergency placements may have disrupted placements because they are more likely to cause emergencies. Carers are presumably more likely to complain of lack of information if things turn out worse than expected. Similarly, young people are less likely to acknowledge they have been consulted over a placement if they are now unhappy in it. Despite these difficulties of interpretation, the researchers who produced these findings tried hard to determine whether they represented cause and effect. On balance they thought this was so. Even if this is not so, there are other reasons for wishing to avoid rush, consult young people, keep carers fully informed and ensure that the importance of previous relationships is respected.

Conclusion

The problems surrounding placing children reflect genuine difficulties. Good practice cannot spirit away the pain of parents or the anxieties of children. There remain issues of balance. Long-term placements face problems associated with undue delay, shorter-term ones are troubled first by rush and then by the difficulties of children overstaying their welcome as suitable longer-term placements are sought. There are genuine balances to be struck between waiting for the perfect match and losing a reasonable chance of permanence. Nevertheless, improvements may be possible.

Some improvements might be made by local authorities who may need to develop placements where carers are prepared to take quite a wide variety of children for varying lengths of time. The variety of criteria against which social workers may need to match (age, length of stay, ethnicity, skill, need to accommodate siblings, geographical considerations and so on) means that the pool of placements can never be large enough to ensure a close match on all criteria. A more feasible strategy is to recruit a pool of carers who can manage a wide variety. Children can then stay until a close match is found.

Other implications relate to direct work with carers:

- Carers should not be subject to pressure to take children whom they do not consider suitable for their families. The CAPS scheme, which did make allowances for carer choice, did not find that this was irresponsibly exercised.[16]

- Carers need information on at least education, health, behaviour and any history of sexual abuse and abusing behaviour, the likely duration of the placement, expected relationships with the child's own family, the child's preferences for food and TV, the child's routines, and other particular things that are important to the child.

- Care should be taken that the information is presented to carers at a time and in such a way that it is easy to absorb. It is not always easy for someone to take in everything in a rush when their attention is focused on introducing a child to their household.

- Where relationships allow this it is probably best for contact between a previous carer and the child to be gradually 'tapered off'.

Yet other implications concern the child:

- The process of making the placement is less difficult for the child if he or she already knows the carers.[1,2,3,11] Placements in which carer and child 'choose each other' are likely to get off to a good start and opportunities for them should not be lightly turned down.

- There should always be a careful assessment of the nature of the relationships between siblings. Work should be carried out on the 'downside' of any plan that is made (e.g. in terms of preparing children for separation and making clear plans for subsequent contact).

- The maximum use should be made of the time available for consultation and sharing information before the placement. Only a minority of the placements defined as emergencies require action within 48 hours.[3]

- There should be recognition of both the limits surrounding consultation and the variety of areas over which it is possible. Children can be given information on a placement, and involved in choices over frequency of contact with parents and other issues, even when the basic issue of whether they should be placed at all cannot be negotiated.

- There should be attention to the things a child takes with him or her to the placement. Such objects can be very important in reassuring the child.[2,13] Sometimes jealous parents or even carers try to deprive them of cherished possessions when they leave[13] and this is a possibility of which social workers should be aware.

There are also implications for work with other services:

- Where children are placed out of county, difficulties in obtaining appropriate educational support for them should be foreseen and agreements struck as to who will arrange and pay for this.

- Formal psychological tests should be used if it is felt that these may strengthen the case for appropriate treatment.

Such developments would need to be matched by training for both carers and social workers. This would have to cover the issues placements raise for young people and their parents, the ways they may express their distress, the kind of response that may help and the importance of previous carers in ensuring the success of a new placement.

The process of placement is fraught and often rushed. All parties may easily misunderstand each other, fail to pass on information, fail to understand information they are given or feel pressured to do things against their better judgement. Questions which arise include:

- Are children and young people consulted over placements as a matter of course?

- Are children given choice over carers where this is possible?

- Are there introductory visits to placements wherever possible?

- Are children consulted over key issues in the placement (e.g. the frequency of visits from particular members of their family)?

- Do social workers make time to work with parents when these decisions are being taken and/or to refer them to independent sources of support?

- Do social workers share all the information they have about a child and do case records allow them readily to find out about past events, such as sexually abusing behaviour, self-harming or school exclusions, which it is crucial to pass on?

Chapter 6

Making Placements Work: The Children

Relationships and effects of fostering within the family vary with the child placed. In very difficult placements it can be a very stressful and unrewarding time for all family members. But other times can be very different. (Foster carer)

[The foster carers] didn't know how I'd react and I were acting right horrible, I wanted to go back with my mum and everything. (Foster child)

Foster care is great, it's what I needed and wanted. (Foster child)

I think she just turned round and said to [foster carer] 'you can't tell me what to do – you're not my mum' and all that. I think it stemmed from there really. (Parent of foster child)

Introduction

Placements work or fail to work for a variety of reasons. Some of the relevant factors are outside the placement. These include the birth family and the school. In this chapter, we concentrate on the contribution of one of the key actors within the placement: the children. Our particular concerns are with the effects on outcomes of what the children want and the nature of the children's needs. In this way the discussion in this chapter leads back to and leads on from the discussion in Chapter 4.

The children

Previous research on placements has concentrated on placement breakdown. This is not a completely objective measure. One person may see a breakdown whereas another may see a 'tactical withdrawal'. In addition the fact that a placement does not break down does not necessarily mean that a child is happy in it.[8,11] That said, the factors that predict a breakdown seem to be much the same irrespective of who defines it. In addition breakdowns, whoever defines them, appear to be associated with a wide range of other 'negative outcomes'. They are therefore a useful marker for the factors that make for difficulty.

Age

The different studies followed the children up for different lengths of time, defined 'breakdown' in slightly different ways, had very different samples of children and defined their age groups in different ways. For these reasons strict comparisons are hard to make. Nevertheless, all studies find that breakdown rates rise with age. It is apparent that:

- The rate of placement breakdowns among those placed when below the age of five is low,[2,11,12,14] probably around 7 per cent among those placed long-term and followed up for 15 years (although the rate of movement among babies can be high for reasons connected with planned moves, carer circumstances, or the failure of placements with parents or relatives[22]).

- Breakdowns are also comparatively rare events among those placed aged 5–11, particularly if the period of follow-up is short, but may rise to around a quarter[12] or above[14] when considered over a 10- to 15-year period.

- Those aged 11 to 15 have much higher rates of placement breakdown with the more recent studies suggesting a rate of around 40 per cent in the first year and around 50 per cent with longer follow-up.[2,3,11,12]

- The rate of breakdown drops somewhat among older teenagers. This may be partly because their period at risk of breakdown is less and partly because difficulties may be resolved by 'planned moves' to independent living.[12]

Clearly, early placement is associated with avoidance of disruption over the longer term and in keeping with this the longer a child has spent in placement the less likely he or she is to disrupt. Length of time in placement is, however, a two-edged sword. The longer the time in placement the older a child becomes, and getting older is associated with risk of disruption.

Child difficulties

Foster children have endured much. Unsurprisingly they often behave in ways others find difficult. One of the core studies compared its sample of children with matched controls in the community. The researchers found that the children who were aged between 5 and 11 were much more likely to score highly on measures of over-activity, conduct and problems with their peers and on a general measure of disturbance. They also showed a wide range of difficult behaviours, some of them varying by age, and some thought to be particularly characteristic of difficult children. These included pestering, over-friendliness to strangers on the one hand (younger children) and stoicism and reluctance to seek comfort on the other (older children). Eating problems were found in a minority of younger children and sexualised behaviour in a minority of older ones. The most significant difficulties were in what were described as over-activity, poor attention and defiance.[8]

Older foster children spend more of their time at school and outside the home. Unsurprisingly they show problems in relation to school and their relationships with the law. Those included in the Scottish study of treatment foster care probably showed the highest levels of such difficulties.[16] Almost none of them, for example, had been able to attend school regularly without very substantial support and eight out of ten had been physically aggressive to others at some point prior to placement.

Some of these difficulties proved highly resistant to change. Four reports[3,11,12,16] measured disturbance at two points in time through a set of questions known as the Strengths and Difficulties Questionnaire. All four reported that there was very little change on this measure. This does not mean that there may not have been other less easily measurable changes – indeed there was evidence that there were.[11] Unsurprisingly, however, carers found continuing problems difficult.

In all age groups emotional or behavioural difficulties, such as hyperactivity at the start of placement, are linked to a lack of stability or to breakdown.[3,7,11,12,13] This is so irrespective of whether the difficulties are displayed within the home or outside it.

Child motivation

We have argued that children want a measure of control over their futures and have a moral right to be consulted. There are also pragmatic reasons for paying attention to what they want. One study[11] found that a simple foster carer rating of whether the foster children 'wanted to be there' strongly predicted outcome over one year. This finding was in keeping with qualitative data from this and other studies. Some foster children say that placements succeed partly because this is what they want.[11,16] Foster carers and social workers similarly stress the importance of the children's motivation. Older children who have accepted their need to be looked after may settle down and get on with it. Those who have not may be seen as 'manipulating a disruption'.[11]

In the study of adolescents[3] three foster children were said to have effectively ended the placement because they wished to live elsewhere.[3] This wish commonly reflects a yearning for home. The importance for foster children of being able to 'close accounts' with their birth families or 'cut their losses' is emphasised from qualitative data in four studies.[3,12,14,16] Obviously not all children wished or needed to do this. For some, however, it was important to be able to say that although they loved their mother to bits they were glad that they no longer lived with her or that they had in other ways 'moved on'.

Other predictive factors

Age, emotional disturbance, difficult behaviour and what the child wanted seemed to be the main characteristics of the child that predicted placement breakdown. They were not the only ones reported. Other factors included the number of previous placement breakdowns,[11] learning disability,[2] the degree to which the child was thought to be institutionalised,[14] and various types of abuse.[7,11,13] One study[3] found that adolescents who had no peer problems had fewer breakdowns, as did those who had not experienced emotional distress.

These associations can be tested in further research. For the moment it would be unwise to make too much of some of them. The number of previous breakdowns helps predict subsequent ones but does not explain why breakdowns occur. Few young children are now 'institutionalised', so findings on institutionalisation are not now so relevant. Findings on 'learning disability' are conflicting and suffer from lack of a precise definition of this impairment.

By contrast there is no reason to doubt the potential relevance of the finding that a history of deprivation and abuse was associated with breakdown.[14] Some studies qualify or fail to repeat this result. One[11] found an association between emotional abuse and breakdown but not between breakdown and other forms of abuse. Two studies[2,3] examine the association between background history and various forms of outcome but do not report associations between outcome and abuse. Two further studies[7,8] found associations between breakdown and a particular form of emotional abuse – a child's experience of being singled out for rejection from among a sibling group. This was particularly likely to be important if the child was not placed with a sibling group[8] or, perhaps, if there were other children left with the birth family.[11]

This rather confusing set of findings can perhaps be summarised as follows:

- There is no reason to doubt the 'bad effects' of abuse. Whether or not abuse predicts breakdown in a sample of foster children will depend on the characteristics of other children in the sample – for example, the number of children who are being looked after because of their difficult behaviour rather than because they have been abused.‡

- The particular difficulties displayed by abused children may well have to do with their prior abuse, whose effects depend on their current context. Sexual abuse and rejection predicted difficult relationships with

---

‡ This may explain why the study of ethnic minority children found an association whereas the study of adolescents did not. Children in the first study who were not abused may have been placed because of their parents' misfortunes. Non-abused adolescents in foster care are likely to have been displaying difficult behaviour.

carers among children placed on their own but not among children placed with siblings.[8]

- The emotional context of the abuse – whether it is perceived as involving 'high criticism and low warmth' – is probably more important in most cases than the actual abusive event. Emotional abuse is strongly associated with other forms of abuse. Three studies also find it associated with outcome.[§]

Two interesting findings from the study of adolescents[3] suggests the paradoxical conclusions that both 'psychological distress' and difficulty in getting on with peers may make children less likely to experience a placement breakdown. There may be two reasons for this. First, children with these difficulties may be less likely to have others – for example, friends – who lead them astray. Second, a capacity to experience psychological distress was apparently related to the capacity to have significant relationships. Those young people who were rated as having close ties with at least one adult were significantly less likely to have placement breakdown and more likely to have experienced emotional or psychological distress. Children who are open to relationships (and hence more vulnerable to relationship difficulties) and look to adults for support are the ones who do particularly well in foster care.

Factors which do not predict breakdown

These findings on 'other factors' point to the limitations of an approach to foster care that concentrates too exclusively on factors that predict breakdown. Physical disability does not predict breakdown – if anything, it does the reverse.[11] It does, however, predict a lengthy period in foster care[2,12] and also has implications for the care the child needs. The fact that, for example, a lack of friends predicts an absence of trouble does not mean that it is to be welcomed. Few would want foster children to grow up and lead lonely, unhappy lives. The three most important factors that do not predict breakdown, or do not do so in a simple way, are gender, ethnicity and disability.

Gender

The core studies have less to say about gender than might be expected. It is not associated with outcome.[11] It is, however, an issue to which foster carers give impor-

---

§ Emotional abuse may be hard to rate on the basis of records alone. This may explain the lack of an association between abuse and outcome in the record-based part of the family contact study. The three studies which found an association sought information from social workers directly.[7,8,11]

tance. Some express strong preferences for taking males or females.[3,10] Some carers are anxious about allegations of sexual abuse and avoid leaving male carers alone with female foster children. One study found that foster carers were significantly less sensitive to the needs and anxieties of adolescent girls than boys.[3] As for the children themselves, female foster children were more likely to have suffered sexual abuse, less likely to get into trouble with the law, and more diligent in their studies.[12] On leaving foster care a number set up households with a baby, something that sometimes brings them back into contact with their own mothers or attracts support from their boyfriend's family.[12] One study suggests that this, for many of them, may be a more viable option than that offered by the vagaries of the job market.[12]

Disability

There were only four reports that included sizeable samples of disabled children.[3,11,12,14] These studies face the usual difficulties of providing precise definitions of degree of impairment and distinguishing impairments from the limitations imposed on those with them by their social context. The results suggested that:

- children who are defined as disabled by one social worker or foster carer are often defined as not disabled by other workers or carers or on different occasions[11]

- most disabled foster children are looked after not because of their disability, although this may be a contributing factor, but for the same reason as others – the existence or risk of abuse

- children who are seen as disabled are less likely than others to return home, less likely to be adopted, more likely to go into residential care and more likely to remain looked after

- disabled young people are more likely than others to remain with their carers after reaching the age of 18. There are, however, difficulties in arranging for the same carers to continue to care for them if this is appropriate when the young people become the responsibility of adult services.

[11] Differences may reflect changes over time (e.g. a child who was seen as difficult is given a diagnosis of autism), different views of the severity of impairment necessary to constitute a disability, the appropriateness of the label for children with conditions which may or may not be seen as 'organic' (e.g. ADHD) or which most would regard as 'psychological' (e.g. attachment disorder) and the relevance of compensatory devices (e.g. very poor sight compensated by very strong glasses).

Ethnicity

The major study of ethnicity is that by Thoburn *et al.*[14] All the children in that study were selected as coming from minority ethnic groups. A number of other studies[1,3,7,11,12] had samples in which the proportion of minority ethnic children varied between 15 per cent[11] and 18 per cent.[13] The size of these other samples meant that with the exception of two of the York samples[11,12] these proportions yielded around 10 to 12 children. They did not therefore allow for statistical generalisation. The larger York samples did provide around 70 children but this was by dint of amalgamating children of very diverse ethnicities. Thoburn *et al.*'s East Anglia study is therefore the only one that has a useful statistical base for talking about ethnicity.

The findings from the core studies include the following:

- The proportion of minority ethnic children recruited to the short-term fostering study was less than would have been expected from the ethnic composition of the areas in which the study took place. The authors suggest that the reason was probably a lack of appropriate publicity to local professionals.[1]

- Ethnic minority children placed with carers from ethnic minorities were no more or less likely to have a placement breakdown than similar children placed with a white British family.[11,14]

- Evidence from the main study of ethnicity suggested that boys from minority ethnic groups were less likely to experience placement breakdown when placed with white families than with parents of similar ethnic background, whereas with girls the reverse was the case. This was a significant difference and the authors recommend that it is tested in further research.[14]

Despite these rather ambiguous results Thoburn *et al.* do not conclude that minority ethnic children could be as well placed with white families as not. They and other researchers argue that:

- Qualitative data make clear the importance of ethnicity to the black and Asian children and the extra difficulties that white carers have in bringing them up.[14]

- Minority ethnic children have to make sense of their histories as foster children from particular ethnic groups. Depending on their circumstances and opportunities for contact with family and other black people they variously worked at these issues or put them 'on the back-burner' awaiting a time when they could turn to them.[14]

- Matching may well need to take account of more subtle characteristics than simply whether child and carer are both from minority ethnic groups. In individual cases other considerations such as religion may be very important.[1,12]

- Such refined matching may be difficult because, for example, the proportion of minority ethnic carers from a particular group may be very small and the chance that they have a vacancy at the time when a particular child from their group has a need may well be low.

- This would suggest that relative carers may have a particular advantage for this group but the proportion of relative carers from ethnic minorities was not, in the core studies, higher than it was among the 'ordinary' foster carers.[10]

Placements were not always ethnically matched and minority ethnic children were under-represented in some studies. In one study boys of minority ethnic origin in ethnically matched placements were more likely to experience disruption than those in placements that were not ethnically matched. With girls the reverse was the case. Other studies found no relationship between ethnicity and breakdown. Ethnicity and placement breakdown are complicated phenomena and simple associations between them are not to be expected. Questions which arise include:

- Is adequate priority given to finding suitable carers from a wide variety of ethnic backgrounds?

- Is the practice of placing children with families of a different ethnic background unusual and clearly linked to specific reasons in individual cases – for example, a strong attachment to an existing carer or the existence of good contact with birth family members to nurture the sense of ethnic pride and identity?

- Where children are not in matched placements do they have access to successful role models from their own ethnic group?

- Does the need to make ethnically matched placements mean that agencies overlook the need to ensure that these placements are also appropriate to the children in other ways?

- Are there barriers to access to 'popular' schemes such as shared care fostering?

Conclusion

These findings suggest that foster carers have to be equipped to deal with two sets of difficulties or needs: those which are likely to lead to a placement breakdown and those which are relevant to the child's well-being. Both need to be taken into account.

The outcomes of placements were influenced by children's characteristics and by their wishes. Children with physical impairments stayed longer in their placements. Difficult and disturbed behaviour was the main reason for placement breakdown, with teenage placements particularly likely to disrupt. Children who did not want to be in the placement were more likely to disrupt. Questions which arise include:

- Absence of breakdown does not mean an absence of unhappiness. Is care taken to find out whether young and disabled children, who are not likely to experience a breakdown, are happy where they are?

- Is consideration given to the needs of long-staying disabled children so that they have access to adoption if appropriate and, if appropriate, continuity of care at the age of 18?

- Are carers trained to deal with difficult behaviours and do they have access to consultation when they encounter them?

- Are there specialist placements for teenagers if needed?

- Where children reach their teenage years in foster care, their carers may benefit from additional training or support. Is this available?

- Is the exploration of what the child or young person wants a central concern in all planning for them, even if it is not always possible to meet these wishes?

- If a foster child wants to go home, do social workers explore the reasons, make return possible with any necessary safeguards or explain why it is not possible and seek, if appropriate, to meet the children halfway?

Chapter 7

Making Placements Work: Foster Families

These people are really nice. I love everyone here, even the animals. (Foster child)

[The foster carers] shout at me all the time and send me upstairs. (Foster child)

I had a couple of bad foster homes but when I found Jane and Mike it all changed. I knew they were the ones for me. I was treated as one of their own. (Foster child)

Foster care is sometimes good and OK, other times horrible, depending where you are. (Foster child)

Introduction

The chances of placement success are to some extent determined in advance. Some children are easier than others. Some foster carers are particularly experienced, committed and skilled. However, there is an also an unpredictable 'chemistry' between the main players in the placement so that placements develop in ways that are hard to foresee. In this chapter we consider the contribution of the foster carers both during and after the placement. We also look at the interactions between the child and the rest of the foster family over the course of the placement. In general we would predict that those carers who are more 'successful' are those who are skilled at providing what the children want – for example, in making them feel at home. They should also be those who are able to meet what children need in terms of commitment, warmth and encouragement from their carers. How far were these expectations fulfilled?

Is it easy to identify good foster carers?

Previous research has explored the characteristics of 'good foster carers'. Some researchers have looked for 'hard', easily identifiable markers.[23] So, successful foster carers have variously been found to be relatives of the child, experienced, and in their forties. Unfortunately other researchers have failed to repeat these findings. What have the core studies to say about them?

The most negative comment on the contribution of foster carers to outcome comes from the study of minority ethnic placements.[14] The authors found that placement breakdown rates did not vary between fostering and adoptive placements, the age or marital status of the foster parents, or between placements that were ethnically matched and those which were not.

This study relied on records for describing the carers. It was therefore limited to 'harder factors', examining, for example, ethnicity rather than styles of parenting. Its finding that harder variables were not related to outcomes was typical of the findings of the core studies. One study[3] did find that carers who had previous relevant experience were more likely to have 'successful' placements, although they were not more likely to avoid breakdowns. The other studies failed to find such associations. We look below at the findings on some of the more easily identifiable characteristics of placements.

Relative placements

Early studies in the United States and England have led to a belief that relative placements are more successful.[23] These studies took place when relative placements may only have been made when there were very strong reasons for them. Such placements are now much more common and recent US studies are much less encouraging. As we discussed earlier, the case for relative placements remains strong. Their results, if no better than, are at least as good as those of other kinds of placement. However, it is also true that they can face particular difficulties, that they typically receive a low level of support and that they need more.

Other children in the placement

Other children in the placement had a potentially key influence on its course. In practice they rarely threatened it. Newly placed children's relationships with the carer's own children were often cool and distant, albeit sometimes marked by low levels of rivalry and jealousy.[3,7] This lack of contact may have helped to prevent serious problems. Young people who separated themselves from other children in the family were less likely to disrupt.[3] Most carers and adoptive parents reported that the impact of the foster or adopted children on their own children was mixed, neutral or good.[3,7,10,11,15]

In the carers' view their own children generally liked, welcomed or at least did not reject the new placement, although commonly they found it more difficult than expected.[8,11,15] Some of these children, like their parents, were very sad when foster children left.[10,15] This generally favourable picture of the relationship between birth and foster or adoptive children is in keeping with the findings of earlier research.[23]

Problems with the carers' own children certainly occur. The researchers reported difficulties over jealousy (even with grown-up children who had left the placement), over the amount of attention given to a foster child, over sharing rooms or possessions, and the destruction or theft of property. The birth child could be led into bad habits or involved in trouble with the police. In extreme cases the birth children might abuse foster children or be abused by them.

Problems with birth or foster children in the placement are associated with disruptions or lack of stability;[3,7,11] they distress other foster children and birth children[7,11,15] and trigger feelings of being treated differently in the foster child concerned.[11,12,13] Adolescents who had a negative impact on others in the household, or who were a physical risk to others, were much more likely to have poor outcomes including disruptions.[3] Carers who found that fostering was difficult for their children were more likely to withdraw from it.[15] Because foster placements with these problems are less likely to last than others, they are less likely to occur in research samples and may seem less frequent than they are.

Earlier research suggested that fostering breakdowns may be more common when there are birth children. In this respect the results of the core studies were mixed. Three[8,11,14] did not find any association between breakdown and the number of other children in the placement. Contrary to early research, explorations of the effect of the age gap between foster and birth children either found no effect[11] or, in the case of adolescents, that a small gap had a good effect.[3] In contrast, Quinton *et al.*[7] found that children placed in families where there were already children did tend to do worse on their measure of stability. It was, however, difficult to be sure whether it was their placement or their pre-existing difficulties (notably rejection by their birth families) that was responsible for their problems.

Case studies and the comments of foster children suggest that these results reflect a mixed picture and that the presence of other children in a placement can cause difficulties but can also help. In keeping with this there is evidence that the effect of other children is influenced by:

- *the age of the children* – younger children spend more time in the placement and in the core studies the association between the number of other children and difficulty in the placement is only reported in younger samples

- *the characteristics of the children* – rejected children placed away from their siblings but with other children may fear the experience of being singled out which they have experienced in their birth families

- *the reaction of the parents* – foster carers are reluctant to take foster children who are very much older than their own.[15] There is some evidence that they are less likely to provide sensitive and committed parenting to a child who joins an existing group of children.[7]

In short there is no simple answer to questions about the effects of other children on a placement. It all depends.

Placement with siblings

The great majority of fostered children have siblings. Their relationships with them are, however, varied. In the study of late sibling placements[8] many children had half-siblings, siblings whom they had never seen or foster siblings unrelated by blood but to whom the children were close. Any definition of 'sibling' might therefore not correspond to the children's emotional world.[8] Many children were desperate to see more of their siblings. For others contact with some siblings was a matter of indifference.

In practice, social workers tried to keep siblings together wherever possible. Frequently, it was not possible to do so. Some children were too old to be in the care system. Some entered it at different times so that it was difficult to place them with siblings who were already looked after. Some interacted with their siblings in ways that made it very difficult to keep them together. Some became separated by accidents of history – for example, one would experience a disruption and another would not. In some cases social workers had to trade the desirability of placing siblings together against the opportunity offered by a suitable placement which could only take some of them.[8,22]

Despite these difficulties the core studies did provide some clear-cut results. These strongly suggest that:

- children placed away from other siblings are more likely to have experienced rejection at home[7,8]
- children who have siblings at home are more likely to experience a disruption than children who have not[11]
- rejected children placed apart from their siblings are less likely to have stable placements than rejected children placed with their siblings[8]
- relationships between siblings can be harmonious and a source of security but can also be very fraught and threaten placements.[8]

Other things being equal, siblings have a right to see each other and be placed together. The effects of this, however, are likely to depend on the relationships between them, whether they want this contact and the reasons for placement.

Parenting styles

Carers, social workers and fostering social workers certainly believe that carers make a difference. In keeping with this view one study[11] found that some carers were consistently more likely than others to experience placement breakdowns.

This finding was not explained by the characteristics of the children. The more successful carers did, however, care in a distinctive way.

Theories about parenting suggest that some styles – particularly authoritative parenting, which combines clear boundaries with warmth – work better than others. In keeping with this, it was found that placements were less likely to disrupt when carers:

- were rated as 'authoritative' (warm, encouraging, clear over expectations etc.)[11]

- took part with their foster children in enjoyable joint activities (e.g. reading a bedtime story or going to a football match)[11]

- were rated as able to respond to the young people in relation to their emotional rather than their chronological age (for example, by providing regular opportunities for play and nurture that was appropriate to a much younger child to meet earlier unmet needs) and the young people said that their carers listened to them and enabled them to talk about their past adverse experiences and current concerns.[3]

Similarly there was evidence that:

- placements were more likely to be rated as successful when the carers were involved in helping the young person to learn independence skills and also when they provided high levels of monitoring of young people's activities outside the placement[3]

- 'unresponsive' carers, particularly those whose parenting tended to be aggressive or otherwise inappropriate, were more likely than others to have placements that were rated as unstable and children whose behaviour deteriorated.[7]

Responsiveness in action

In practice it was not easy to be authoritative. Foster children could be difficult but also quick to sense rejection. The problem was how to provide clear guidance without undermining the child's self-respect or making her or him feel rejected.

Qualitative data in the study of specialist foster care[16] suggested that this dilemma could be overcome. In the most successful placements in that study, carers concentrated on relationships and on flexible problem-solving within the context of a relationship that was expected to endure. They also needed to work with parents – usually avoiding criticism, and facilitating contact, while nevertheless encouraging the young person to take a realistic if sympathetic attitude.

The York studies[10,11,12] similarly suggested that what was necessary was a capacity to combine clear limits with empathy and an assurance that the child would not be rejected. The researchers suggested that carers needed to:

- handle attachment appropriately by:
  - dealing sensitively with previous attachments and losses
  - offering security with persistence and avoiding threats of rejection
  - offering tolerable closeness
  - showing sensitivity to attachment times and approaches
  - dealing sensitively with feelings of jealousy and exclusiveness
  - going out of their way to make the child feel at home
- reinforce socially acceptable esteem and identity by:
  - praising success of whatever kind
  - not dwelling on failure
  - setting realistic expectations
  - maintaining a positive but realistic picture of the child
- handle difficult behaviour appropriately by:
  - analysing reasons/motives for behaviour
  - avoiding increasing these motives
  - setting clear limits
  - negotiating with the child in ways that avoided humiliating him or her
  - offering alternative ways of meeting needs
  - avoiding the reinforcement of difficult behaviour
  - reinforcing competing behaviour.

Good and bad spirals

Relationships between carers and children show both stability and change over time. Quinton *et al.*[7] provide the most detailed account of how this occurs. Their account emphasises the contribution of both child and carer to this process. In their study:

- The child's characteristics had a major influence on parenting style. Carers found it particularly difficult to respond sensitively to children who had been rejected.
- The more problems the child presented the less easy the carers found it to be responsive and the more likely it was that their parenting would deteriorate over time.
- Deterioration in the child's behaviour was generally accompanied by a worsening in her or his relationship with the carers but some carers remained strongly committed to the child despite this change for the worse.
- Placements were most likely to go well when the child was placed with her or his own siblings, was not over-active and was looked after by a responsive carer.

Responsive parenting seemed to be most important when the child was over-active or had been rejected by her or his parents. The responsiveness did not reduce the difficult behaviour. Responsive carers were, however, much more committed to the children and likely to form a relationship with them.

There were similar results from the study of adolescents.[3] Those who settled early in the placement, confided in their carers and enjoyed activities with them tended to do well.[3] Those who developed new problems over drugs, alcohol or risky sexual behaviour tended to do badly.[3] Carers who were initially optimistic and satisfied with the placement tended to have success. Those who reduced their efforts at control or became more or less aggressive, less warm or less committed had less success. As relationships deteriorated so good outcomes became less likely.

One study[11] developed a measure of 'rejection', which largely reflected the way the child was seen. As in Quinton et al.'s study[7] rejection was more likely when the child was 'difficult' but was not automatic. Apparently difficult children who were not rejected were no more likely to have a placement disruption than others.

So the overall message is that both child and carer contribute to the outcome. Each may bring out the best or worst in the other. In the end, the outcome of the placement depends on the relationship that develops.

Carer strain

It would seem likely that foster carers who are strained would be less likely to perform in a skilled and committed way. Three studies[3,7,11] looked specifically at whether strained carers were less successful than others.

The study of adolescents[3] showed that very high strain prior to placement was linked to high disruption levels, that strain on carers during placement was linked to worsening parenting skills and that this in turn linked to more disrupted placements. Carers who had four or more stressors in the six months prior to placement were judged less likely to seek appropriate help for young people or help them fit into the foster family and were less likely to feel supported. Those who reported 'being under strain' were less likely to be rated as committed to the child, as engaged with them, as providing sensitive parenting, as liking the young people, responding to their emotional age, preparing them for leaving or providing beneficial placements. By follow-up, these strained carers were also less likely to provide effective limits. Another study[11] found that strained carers were more likely to have experienced allegations and disruptions in the past. Moreover, at any given level of 'child difficulty', strained carers were more likely to experience a placement disruption over the coming year than less strained carers.

Quinton et al.[7] distinguished between different sources of stress on carers. Some were related to the placement – for example, the anxiety of waiting to know whether an adoptive placement would be approved. Others were related to difficult behaviour of the child. Some were related to other factors – for example, changes in work outside the home. Unsurprisingly, feelings of strain related to the child were much more common when the child was behaving in a difficult way. The other sources of stress did not appear to be related to the progress of the placement.

These findings raise questions of cause and effect. Are carers under strain at least partly because they are not naturally as fitted for being a carer as others? Alternatively, are they caring less well because they are under strain? In practice this question is rather academic. Irrespective of the effect on outcomes it is not desirable for carers to be under strain. It is also hard to believe that carers who are under strain care as skilfully as they would in other circumstances or that they are as committed to their foster children.

Does training influence outcomes?

The findings suggest that skilled, unstressed carers are more likely to have good results. This in turn suggests that performance should be improved by training and support. How far do the core studies support this conclusion?

The specialist fostering scheme[16] provided the most systematic approach to the training and support of carers described in the core studies. This scheme proved able to contain some very difficult young people, many of whom either came from secure accommodation or would otherwise have needed it. Unfortunately, it was not possible to tell which particular aspects of the scheme were crucial to this achievement.

In general the studies provide plenty of evidence that carers appreciate training,[1,3,10,15,16] although either they or the researchers were generally able to point out gaps, practical difficulties and ways in which the training could be improved.[2,3,10,15] Despite this praise the studies provided little evidence that current training has much effect on outcomes:

- One study[11] found no evidence that the number of hours of training a carer had received was related to outcomes.

- The study of adolescent fostering[3] found that training in 'letting children go' and over contact with parents were associated with 'placement success' but not with the avoidance of disruption.

- Cleaver[2] reported that carers with formal training on contact were more likely to have established positive relationships with parents and to be involved in contact arrangements. Numbers, however, were too small for a test of significance and the carers themselves did not usually see the training as relevant to their problems with contact.

- The major experimental study of training in behavioural methods failed to show a significant effect.[6]

This evidence on the effectiveness of training is at least comparable in strength to that on the effectiveness of training for social workers or residential workers. Nevertheless, the evidence is sparse and inconclusive. Thus, while the payment of foster carers is developing on the assumption that training justifies greater financial rewards, presumably on the grounds that it is linked to effectiveness,[5] the evidence for this association is lacking. The point is not that there is an alternative to developing a well-trained workforce. It is rather that is unsafe to assume that any particular form of training will 'work' or that, even if it does, its effectiveness may not depend on other changes that need to go with it.

Does support influence outcomes?

The strongest evidence for the impact of support on outcomes comes from the study of adolescent fostering. This looked at both informal support from family and friends and more formal support from social workers, counsellors and other workers in mental health. It found that successful placements were more likely when:

- young people were receiving counselling
- social workers arranged services for the young people
- foster carers were supported by their immediate family, or received 'useful' support from their social networks or from local professionals. Support from their parents and children was particularly crucial for lone carers
- foster carers received useful support from the young people's social workers.

There were some associations between placement breakdown and the experience of seeking or receiving support. Young people who were thought to be receiving 'appropriate therapeutic help' were less likely to experience a placement breakdown. Those whose carers sought mental health help for them because it had not been forthcoming were more likely to disrupt. In addition, carers who received a lot of support from their own children (including adult children who lived at home or nearby) had fewer disruptions.

In general carers who felt poorly supported were more likely to feel under strain and to be exposed to difficult behaviour on the part of the young people for which they felt that appropriate help was not forthcoming. They found social workers difficult to contact, might feel that asking for help was discouraged, and were likely to be dissatisfied with at least one of the set of formal services on offer. Carers who received high levels of support from their children were more likely to have successful placements and children whose behaviour improved. Carers with overall high levels of support were more likely to be rated as showing warmth and as having young people whose needs had been met.

These findings can be contrasted with other less encouraging ones. Quinton *et al.*[7] found no association between the amount of social work support given to placements and their outcomes. They attributed this partly to the rather generalised and unspecific nature of this support (see also Rushton *et al.*[8]). York study 2[11] found that the provision of almost any kind of help, with the exception of educational psychology, was associated with disruption. The explanation seemed to be that help was targeted on children in difficulty. However, the findings did not suggest that currently available specialist services are adequate in either quantity or quality to prevent disruption.

In practice associations in this area are difficult to interpret. The researchers in the adolescent fostering study[3] found associations between low levels of social work visiting and telephone contact and stress, and between stress and breakdowns. They interpreted this as suggesting that social work support reduces breakdown. Two of the York studies[11,12] found a similar association between stress and breakdown; they also found that perceived poor support from social workers went with disruption. They argued, however, that foster carers in difficulties might take a gloomy view of everything or blame the social workers, who in turn might criticise them. The results were not conclusive. However, these researchers concluded that a perceived lack of support from social workers was more probably a consequence of a placement going wrong than a cause of it.

Associations between perceived levels of support and successful outcomes are also inconclusive. Carers in placements that are going wrong may be more likely to perceive themselves as ill supported. Similarly, an association between the provision of counselling and success could show that one affects the other. Alternatively, children may only be willing to accept counselling if they are seriously trying to 'get their heads in order'.

Given these uncertainties the general conclusions would therefore seem to be:

- Perceptions of a lack of formal and informal support go with negative spirals in placements. They may or may not cause these spirals. They are undesirable on any grounds.

- The evidence suggests that the usual levels of contact with mental health professionals do not affect outcomes.

- Possible exceptions to this rule are provided by counselling and educational psychology, but the evidence on their effectiveness cannot be regarded as conclusive.

- Inadequate social work support is associated with carer strain, may for this reason contribute to increasing difficulties in placement and poorer outcomes and should, in any event, be deplored.

- Specific, high-quality interventions need to be developed to prevent negative spirals and their effectiveness tested.

Conclusion

The findings on 'matching' are complex and difficult to convey in a clear way. Rigid rules about age gaps, the presence of carers' children and the like are not justified by research and restrict choice. They do, however, generally point to key issues that need to be considered.

On balance the evidence does not support a blanket rule against placing foster children in families with birth children. It does suggest a need for careful exploration and monitoring. Potential foster children, foster carers and children already in the family are likely to have views about the wisdom of inviting a particular foster child to join a family group. These views are important. Social workers should also be cautious about placing children who have been rejected or who are sensitive to being 'the odd one out' in placements where there are already other children.

Similar issues are raised by the placement of siblings. Other things being equal siblings should clearly be placed together if this is what they want. Nevertheless, relationships within sibling groups should always be carefully assessed.[8] If siblings cannot be kept together it may still be possible to keep them in close touch; it may also be possible to acknowledge the meaning the separation has for a child and work to counter the possible sense of rejection this brings with it.

So it is dangerous to say simply 'Do not bother about the age gap' or 'Separate siblings'. It is, however, possible to weigh the risks and decide to place more children in a placement than might seem desirable without ill effects. In this way and by, for example, making grants for extensions, a local authority may both increase choice and the number of placements available.

Other findings in this chapter are less complicated. Outcomes depend heavily on foster carers, the children in the household and their reaction to the foster child. Foster families who provide 'authoritative' and 'responsive' parenting are less likely to experience breakdowns. Families are more likely to react negatively to challenging children, particularly if their behaviour is seen as damaging to other family members. Such reactions are not, however, inevitable. If families do not respond to difficult behaviour with rejection the placement does not break down. The problem is how to develop forms of training and support which help the carer to parent in a skilled way and prevent negative spirals from developing. At present no English study has demonstrated successful ways of doing this.

The outcome of placements depends heavily on the foster carers, other children in the placement and the way all members of the family 'get on' with the foster child. The research does not support rigid rules of thumb about, for example, age gaps between children in the household. It does suggest that issues such as age gaps or placement with siblings are very important to individual children. Good or bad spirals can develop in which relationships between members of the family improve or deteriorate. The questions arising include:

- Is there careful assessment that takes into account the views of the foster family and the views and needs of the child?

- Are children, particularly if made scapegoats at home, placed with their siblings where possible? Are sibling relationships a focus for work both for those placed together and those apart?

- Are birth children given opportunities to seek support without burdening their parents or appearing to criticise them?

- Is training informed by evidence on the needs and wishes of foster children and the characteristics of successful foster carers?

- Are social workers willing to end placements that are not working or convert short-stay placements into long-stay ones if this seems appropriate?

- Are foster carers supported at the beginning of 'negative spirals' and before these become entrenched?

Chapter 8

Making Placements Work: Birth Family and Contact

[I like it that] they still let me go and stay with my mum and see my nan and grandad, and see my auntie, uncle and nephew. (Foster child)

The social worker I have at the moment won't leave me to get on with the family I am with. She keeps offering to arrange meetings with my own family. (Foster child)

This stupid b*t*h [social worker] did her best to make sure we wouldn't get contact with our younger sisters. She switched my words around, turning our family against each other. (Foster child)

What I like about foster care is that I feel like I have two families. (Foster child)

Introduction

Children and foster carers are not the only people who make a placement work. Outside, the child's own family and school play crucial roles. This chapter focuses on the child's own family and, more specifically, on contact. Birth families have needs in their own right and these cannot be wrapped up under the single heading of 'contact'. Contact, however, is undeniably important. It is also an issue on which the research has much to say.

At a general level the child's family are clearly likely to be central to the child's needs and wishes and to the principles outlined in Chapter 4. They are the most likely source of close relationships as well as of damaging ones. They may meet needs or give rise to needs that have to be assuaged. They are a potential source of identity, one that has to be affirmed, modified or given up. The children's view of their families helps to determine the degree to which they want to be in the placement. Change or lack of change in the family may determine the long-term outcomes of the children who return there. Where the child cannot return, he or she has to face the reasons for this and psychologically 'move on'.

Birth families and contact

The most detailed study of contact was that by Cleaver.[2] She found that foster children were often preoccupied with their families and with the reasons for their placement. Both children and parents commonly spent time thinking about each other every day.[2]

Work could be done on these issues without face-to-face contact: for example, through counselling the child or working with the family on their own. Treasured possessions, photographs, special activities or rituals could serve to keep the sense of connection alive. Parents and child could telephone each other and sometimes did so frequently. Letters were rarely used in this way but could be highly prized.[2] In practice, however, the most common means of communication were meetings between family and child. (We call them 'contacts' for short.)

As is well known, views on face-to-face contact have changed. Before World War II the common approach was to discourage contact. Vestiges of this approach probably continued into the 1980s. Now, however, the need for contact is embodied in legislation and widely accepted by social workers and carers.[2] Children, it is believed, need contact with parents so that the latter can 'give permission' for the new carers to parent, and so that the children do not develop unrealistic fantasies, have a basis for their 'identity' and a resource available to them in later life. Research has suggested that contact is associated with a greater likelihood of return home and good mental health but that it is prevented by poor practice and avoidable difficulties.[23] Cleaver's research[2] was commissioned partly to investigate how such problems might be overcome.

Characteristics of contact

Contact is now much more frequent than has been the case in the past. In the core studies between 40 and 50 per cent of foster children had at least weekly contact with at least one family member.[2,3,11] All the studies agreed that where the mother was alive she was the most likely person to be in contact. The next most prominent group were siblings outside the placement (contact with the mother often involves contact with them). Fathers, grandmothers, aunts and uncles all provided some contact but less frequently than the other groups.[2,3,11] Distant placements faced parents with difficulties over cost, transport and journey times.[2] As found in earlier studies, the frequency of contact was strongly associated with distance[11] and prohibitions on contact.[11]

Age was also an important factor in determining the nature of contact. Adolescents were able to manage the practicalities of contact for themselves. However, this exposed them to high levels of unsatisfactory and sometimes harmful contact. Attention may need to be given to this in work with the family and boundaries placed around detrimental contact.[3]

The extent of contact can vary over time, although early patterns of contact tend to predict later ones.[2,3] The study of adolescents reported that on average it slightly increased, with 30 per cent of the adolescents having more of it and 22 per cent less.[3] Cleaver reported a small (7%) decrease in the prevalence of contact over time, although in her study too there could be increases.[2] The age of the child may well be important in affecting the degree of contact since older children can more easily take the initiative. Thoburn et al.,[14] reporting on earlier practice and a much longer time span, found that adolescents and young adults often sought out contact when it had been allowed to lapse. This was sometimes associated with a quarrel with the carers and sometimes with curiosity and a desire to understand their origin and roots.

Only a minority of between one in six and one in seven children were in touch with no relative at all.[2,3,11] These low levels of contact occurred for various reasons including poor previous attachments,[2] failed adoptions,[3] lengthy periods in the care system[3] or sexual abuse[2,3] which meant that the child was either excluded from the family or excluded her- or himself.[3]

Less seemed to be done about these isolated children than might have been expected. None of the isolated young people in the adolescents study had contact with an independent visitor.[3] Other relatives might be an additional source of contact. In Cleaver's study a sizeable number wished to have contact with additional relatives but few of these had made their wishes known.[2]

The general frequency of contact raises the question of its purpose. In the past contact has been justified on the grounds of its effect on the child's return home. However, in the study of adolescents nearly half the adolescents had weekly contact but only a quarter were returning home. There was a similar contrast in one of the York studies which found regular weekly contact for 44 per cent of the sample but definite plans to return home for only 15 per cent.[11] In that study the most common reasons for contact given by social workers was not to enable a return home but simply to maintain the relationship and to respect the wishes of parents and child.

As might be expected the most detailed account of social work purposes is provided by Cleaver's study.[2] In her qualitative study she compared the main purposes of contact as judged by the social worker with her own assessment of their feasibility. She found that the main purposes were to enable return home, to keep a child in touch, to improve the relationship and to reassure the child. The realism of these ambitions varied:

- Out of nine cases where it was intended to return the child home, the researchers questioned whether this was a realistic objective in seven of them – mainly on the ground that the relationship was poor. Many of these cases involved parents who were mentally ill and the aim of return may have had an element of sympathy.

- In 11 cases the aim was to keep in touch – this was usually realistic, albeit not necessarily at the frequency proposed. In these cases relationships with parents were usually poor, the main source of support might be the foster carer but some form of shared care might sometimes be appropriate.

- In ten cases the primary aim was to improve relationships – this was not realistic if the relationship was poor and therapeutic help was not provided.

- In three cases the aim was to reassure. This was generally realistic. (Reassurance may be particularly necessary for children who have taken responsibility for parents or siblings, for those who see their placement as a rejection or in cases where there have been important changes at home – something experienced by half the young people in the adolescent study.)

The purposes of contact may help to determine where it takes place. The main venues seemed to be the child's home, the social services office and the foster home, with the child's home being the most likely venue and the other two settings equally likely.[2,15] Older children were more likely to go to the birth family's home – a finding that reflects their greater capacity to manage transport and lower concerns about their safety. Younger children and those whose visits had to be supervised were less likely to go to the parental home.[2]

Cleaver reports on views on these different settings.[2] Other things being equal, contact at the birth family's home was preferred by children and parents – it allowed contact with friends and relatives, kept children abreast of changes at home, strengthened family identity and allowed parents to play a meaningful role in children's lives. In contrast, where contact at home did not go well children felt trapped, and although the foster carer commonly knew this, the social worker might not. Children were generally happy for contact to take place in the foster home but parents found that this awakened feelings of loss, guilt and made them feel deskilled. Contact in a social services venue was generally seen as inhibiting and associated with feelings of being watched, although it sometimes allowed the children to feel safe. Contact in prison or in hospital was more popular than might have been expected.

The effects of contact

The overall picture of the effects of contact is complicated. Children usually look forward to contact, commonly want more contact than they get but are nevertheless commonly upset by it.[2,11] Carers and social workers are more satisfied with contact when it is frequent: but this may be partly because they discourage contact with which they are dissatisfied. Improvement in family relationships may reflect an increase in contact: but it may also involve a decrease as young people give up impossible hopes for what their family may be.[16] At some points contact may be a psychological necessity, something which is necessary to quell unbearable longing or bring reality to a distorted picture. At others it may be best put on the back-burner.[14]

Most foster carers accepted the need for contact and in more than four out of ten cases they wished the children had more contact. Their emotions, however, tended to be stirred by difficult aspects of contact rather than the positive ones. Most took up fostering to work with children rather than with their parents.[15] Stressful contacts might involve violence and drunkenness and could deter carers from allowing contact in their homes.[15] Carers reporting them had high levels of mental ill-health.[10] More common problems included unreliability, the impact on children of rejecting parental behaviour and the propensity of parents to try to undermine the carer's discipline, set the child against the carers or expose the child to what were seen as undesirable ways of life or even abuse.[3,11,12] Around a quarter of the carers in the adolescent study said that they or their families were negatively affected by contact.[3] In one study[11] only four out of ten carers were satisfied with the arrangements and around a fifth were dissatisfied or very dissatisfied with them.[11]

A number of researchers either made their own ratings of the effect of contact or asked others to do so. This exercise confirmed the potential of contact for good or harm. Quinton *et al.* asked social workers to assess the impact of contacts with birth mothers in the year prior to placement. Out of 22 such contacts only 6 were seen as being predominantly positive.[7] At the second interview in the adolescent study 69 per cent of the young people were rated as having positive contact with someone and 63 per cent as having detrimental contact. One in four was assessed as suffering from lack of contact with someone who was important to them. Poor contact was seen as contributing to breakdown in a number of cases and rated as being a major cause of breakdown in a fifth of the cases where this occurred.

Statistical associations conveyed a similar picture. In general there was no evidence that *on average* the quantity of contact was associated with good or bad outcomes.[11] It was, however, strongly associated with return home. In the short run this probably reflected the fact that return was most likely when relationships were good (frequent contact was associated with a good previous attachment between mother and child[2]) and return was planned.[11] If this was not so, it would be expected that barriers to contact – and distance was a strong barrier – would have prevented the child from returning. There was no evidence that distance had this effect.[11] In the longer term continued contact may have led to unpredicted returns, allowing them to be considered when there were breakdowns.[12]

There was, however, evidence that contact with specific people could be harmful in certain cases. In the study of adolescents 'detrimental contact' was associated with a lack of beneficial placements but not with breakdown.[3] However, difficulties with contact were associated with higher disruption rates.

Two of the York studies[11,12] suggested that the effects of contact depended in part on whether the child had previously been abused. Where there was strong evidence that the child had been abused prior to placement, prohibitions on contact were associated with better outcomes. In these cases breakdown was three times more likely if, according to the foster carers, all members of the child's family could see the child than was the case if someone was prevented from doing so.[11] Previously abused children with no restrictions on family contact were also more likely to be re-abused either during contact or after return home.[12] These findings seemed to hold for all kinds of abuse and could not be explained through the characteristics of the children, insofar as the researchers were able to take these into account.

The York findings need to be confirmed in other studies. There is, however, enough evidence from all the studies to show that contact can, in some circumstances, do harm. The harm is, however, associated with particular people, not contact in general. The children themselves were sometimes quite specific about which relatives they wished to see and the nature of the contact they wanted with them. So it was possible to want unrestricted contact with a grandmother, never to see a stepfather again, have supervised contact with a mother and talk to other siblings on the telephone.

Contact with particular individuals can also help. Contact with grandmothers seemed particularly beneficial. In the study of adolescents it was associated with a variety of positive indicators.[3] The need for contact with siblings still seemed to be less appreciated than it might be.[7,8] In some cases it fell by default. In others it might bring the child into contact with undesirable lifestyles or lead to contacts with harmful or less welcome relatives. Ways round these problems (e.g. through 'letterbox' arrangements) did not appear to be routinely considered, although in practice all kinds of contact including letterbox contact carry risks. The key is, perhaps, to take a wide view of the nature of possible contact but to consider each kind of contact in relation to its purposes and the individual child involved.

The importance of contact was also underscored by its relevance to the future. Two of the York studies[11,12] found that success on return home was predicted by the joint wish of parent and child for this outcome. This in turn was strongly associated with frequency of contact.[12] In Cleaver's intensive sample[2] successful returns were apparently promoted by purposeful, planned, well-paced, well-resourced and reviewed contact, supported by parental motivation, a positive child response to increased contact and a good attachment between parent and child. So contact is an indicator of the likelihood of a successful return and quite possibly an ingredient (although not the only ingredient) in bringing this success about.

Conclusion

Contact is not the only mechanism for family work. Work with the foster child or with the family on its own is also important. Nevertheless, contact remains a key issue. Unfortunately, work related to it is time-consuming for social workers.[2] It may therefore be skimped. In addition social workers may sometimes be reluctant to take decisions over contact in advance of a court ruling.[22]

In general, contact is a right of children and families. It should only be hindered or prevented if there are good reasons to do so. In practice most children want more of it and evaluate social workers in terms of their ability to promote it.[12] Parents in general are similarly preoccupied with their children and value social workers who keep them in touch.[2] Contact is thus not only about enabling a child to return home – in many cases this is an unrealistic objective. A wide view needs to be taken about its potential and a lively eye kept to its dangers.

Patterns of contact are established early in the placement. They probably need to be a focus of work in the first three months. Arrangements are likely to be easier if contact is seen as part of more general work with the family. This may include work with parents on the trauma of separation or arranging for this to happen. It can also involve encouraging parents to talk over the child with a carer, an opportunity they generally value.[2]

Over this time it is important that the social worker:

- makes a realistic assessment of the attachment between mother and child[2]

- thoroughly assesses both the potential benefits and the risks of contact with a variety of relatives (for example, relationships between siblings vary considerably and should be taken into account in contact plans)[2,3,8,11]

- specifies the purpose of contact, desired frequency and who should be involved (school hours may make it difficult for middle-year children to maintain contact with parents if contact depends on social workers who work office hours, and account should be taken of this)[2]

- involves parents and children in discussing arrangements about contact (at present such discussions with parents only seems to happen in about a third of the cases)[2]

- deals with the issue of venue (other things being equal, children and their parents prefer to meet in their own home and this should be the first option considered but child, parent(s) and carer are all likely to have views on this).[2]

Where there are problems in arranging contact it may be important for social workers to:

- remember the virtues of indirect contact[2]

- introduce new relatives where the relationship is or could be positive[2,3]

- maintain relationships with separated siblings when desired[2,8]
- be aware of the practical and other barriers to contact which parents may face and work to overcome these as necessary.[2]

Two studies[2,3] suggest that contact should provide a chance for therapeutic work. This could provide those children who have experiences of continued rejection by their parents with an opportunity to work through their feelings about this in order to enable them to move on and make use of more beneficial relationships.[3] Contact is sometimes intended to improve relationships between parent and child, but this is rarely associated with therapeutic work. This may be a missed opportunity.[2]

The research suggests that over time it is important to make regular reviews of contact arrangements.[2] For this reason social workers should try to enable the children to talk to them about contact.[2] (Children may not know the social worker, dislike the social worker or be unable to contact the social worker.) They should also be aware that only a minority of children seem to talk easily about the emotions aroused by contact.[2] Foster carers and social workers need to share information since either may be aware of issues over contact when the other is not.[2] Where matters do not seem to be working out it may be possible to undertake imaginative work on the issue (e.g. by changing frequency and venue, or providing an independent visitor).[3]

These issues need to be covered in the training of carers as well as social workers. Carers who have undergone training related to contact tend to have better relationships with child and parents and play a role in contact arrangements.[2] The shared care study amply demonstrated the potential for carers to work with birth families.[1] The extension of this approach to include 'through care' would depend on the ability of carers to include parents as well as children in their work.

Contacts may be beneficial or harmful. Often the same child may have both kinds of contact. Questions that arise include:

- Is a thorough assessment made of the purpose of contact, where it should take place, with whom it is appropriate, whether it should be supervised, how frequent and long it should be and how it should be supported?
- Are children, parents and foster carers involved in these assessments and able to contribute to them?
- Are these assessments reviewed?
- Is the distress felt by children and parents at their separation recognised so that it is not disabling?
- When children are exposed to repeated negative contact experiences is the social worker aware of this and is action taken to deal with it?
- Is contact in particular and foster care more generally seen in the context of work with both child and family?

Chapter 9

School and Education

I used to be picked on all the time at school… [I was unhappy] all the time but then I thought, well stuff this, I'm not letting them stand here and hit me, so I beat one of the ringleaders. (Foster child)

I didn't want to go to college when I was at my mum's house. I didn't even want to study at all. But now I really want to study… I really miss my homework. Do you know that? I actually do. I actually miss it. I used to love my homework. (Former foster child)

The first three years at school was all right… The last two years at school, I spent my whole time just walking around and going to the music room. (Former foster child)

Introduction

Previous research[23] has highlighted the poor educational performance of foster children at school. It has also explored how far this could be seen as a consequence of the care system. In general it suggested that the children were behind at school before they were looked after. The care experience did not on average make their performance better or worse, although differences between the educational performance of children in different residential homes suggested scope for improvement. Children who performed poorly at school also tended to have more difficulties when they left the care system. These findings emphasised the importance of education, which other research suggested was somewhat neglected by social workers.[2]

Partly because of this research current policy emphasises the importance of school. Examination results form the basis of one of the key indicators of local authority performance. As we have seen earlier, the core studies confirmed the importance of education in the provision of placements. School featured prominently in children's accounts of what was important in placements. It was also central to our analysis of their needs. So this would seem to be an area where policy, research and the views of foster children coincide. This chapter explores the findings of the core studies on school in more detail.

Evidence from the core studies

The CAPS researchers argued that 'It would be difficult to overstate the importance of education in this project' (p.161).[16] This statement was amply supported by the other research.

School for foster children in the core studies was much more than a route to academic success or otherwise. It provided structure to the day.[16] It was a place where they must cope with the potential stigma of 'being in care',[1] with the fact that their name was not the same as that of their carers[14] or with the fact that they were conveyed to school in unusual ways.[13] It could be a means of keeping in touch with friends from their former lives.[2] For black children in white families it could be an important source of role models and of contacts with black children.[14] Generally, schools were important as potential sources of self-esteem and as places where children tried out their social wings and got in with the 'right' or 'wrong' crowd.[12,14] Black children formerly in long-term placements similarly placed great importance on school whether for good or ill.[14]

In keeping with the importance of school difficulties, they were associated with problems in the placement and elsewhere. Foster children who were unhappy at school,[11,12] or who truanted from it or were excluded,[3] tended to show other difficulties. Young people of school age but not at school placed carers under considerable strain.[5,16] Conversely, young people who were confident about their schoolwork were less likely to have a placement breakdown.[3] Similarly, young people with particular skills and interests (which may have been developed at school or home) were more likely to have successful placements.[3] So too were those who were confident in social relationships.[3]

Unfortunately, the foster children displayed a wide range of difficulties at school both prior to and after arrival. In the CAPS study only six children had been able to attend school without extensive support[16] before the project. In one study[3] nearly 50 per cent of the young people had been excluded from school, 20 per cent were permanently excluded and around 20 per cent had special educational needs. Just under two thirds were attending ordinary schooling, but of these 30 per cent had attendance problems when first fostered and around half were showing very difficult behaviour there. Despite such problems children were more likely to attribute their poor school performance to their previous experience than to the care system.[13]

Despite this endorsement there was a variety of difficulties over providing good education in the care system. Some of these were associated with frequent movement. Protracted spells in one school were apparently rare,[13] and unscheduled changes of school common.[3] Placement itself involved a change of school for around a third[2] to a half[11] of the foster children studied. It could be difficult for a placing authority to arrange appropriate education in a new authority.[16] Moves of school meant that the children had to make new friends, and take up the curriculum at a different point. For these reasons they were disliked. Sometimes they were avoided by the use of taxis. The consumer study found that these special forms of transport were often a source of embarrassment to the children, although some children welcomed the chance to remain at the same school.[13]

An additional problem was that not all foster carers or social workers attributed great importance to school[3,9,11] or, if they did, found it easy to promote education. In the adolescent study half the foster carers had little involvement with schools.[3] In just under half the cases in this study there was no information on the files on school career. So the general impression was that only 'proactive carers' were likely to fight the child's corner over school. Where foster carers were committed to promoting education this was not always easy for them. Some also complained that their own role in schooling was unclear. Should it be they or the social worker who went to the parents' evening? One study reported that a social worker had told one foster carer that it was not the carer's job to arrange a meeting with the school;[9] another that foster carers sometimes experienced schools as too eager to exclude foster children.[5]

One study found that contact with an educational psychologist was associated with avoidance of placement breakdown.[11] This unpredicted finding was not explained by the characteristics of children seeing the psychologist. There was some evidence that the effects depended on the attitude of the carer and the attitude of the child. Where neither carers nor child had a positive attitude towards school the effect was not apparent. Whatever its explanation this finding reinforced other evidence that doing well at school is of value for its own sake and because of its contribution to placement success.

Success at school is not sufficient to guarantee success at work. For a small minority success at school can lead on to university, continuing support from local authorities and the foundation for a new life.[12] In contrast, school performance may not be associated with happiness and well-being among other care leavers.[12] McDonalds and Pizza Hut perhaps call for other attributes than academic success. The CAPS researchers[16] lamented the lack of good work experience placements. Whatever their school experience hardly any of those graduating out of their scheme seemed to acquire paid work.

Conclusion

In general the research strongly reinforces the case for giving priority to children's education but also underlines the difficulty of doing so. It also suggests that education has to be viewed widely. Children's happiness and social development are at least as important as their academic success. Schools have a major impact on these less academic aspects of life.

Academic achievement at school could, in theory, lead to later success at work. Encouragement of such achievement needs to be accompanied by support for young people over work. It is simply inconsistent to emphasise the need for young people to acquire GCSEs or A levels and then fail to provide them with the support they need to get themselves solidly established in good jobs. Many foster children are never going to be qualified for jobs requiring academic qualifications and their long-term support into the job market is of equal importance.

A variety of related points can be made:

- Education builds on previous progress. Given their low starting point major efforts may be needed to ensure foster children achieve educational success.

- Professionals should take a wide view of the role of schools in a foster child's well-being. It is important that a child is happy at school. This is of value in itself and probably contributes to the success of the placement and to academic success.[11,12]

- In some cases a child has flourished at a particular school and every effort should be made to ensure continuity at it. In other cases this continuity may be less important or a change of school can provide the opportunity for a fresh start.[3]

- Foster carers should ground their efforts to encourage attendance and good school performance in an understanding of why a particular child may not attend. For example, the child may be embarrassed at having to arrive in a taxi, may be being bullied, may lack friends, may be struggling with an unfamiliar curriculum and so on. Efforts to improve the situation need to take account of the particular factors involved.

- Carers and those who train them should consider the work done by the CAPS carers in their work with schools. This included regular weekly contact with schools, the development of strategies for getting the child up on time and to school with the right equipment and clothes, helping the young people find new ways of dealing with anger, spotting potential flash points at school and working out ways round them, encouraging discussion of school and generally fostering the child's self-confidence. All this involved considerable work with the school.[3]

- The evidence of the good effects of an educational psychologist is not conclusive. It is, however, important. There should be experimental work to determine whether the routine involvement of these psychologists in, say, developing educational plans for foster children is able to enhance their attendance, happiness at school and academic performance.[11]

- The child's happiness at school is equally important when he or she returns home. The lessons learned in foster care should be applied to this more difficult situation (e.g. in terms of providing support to parents over how to help their children educationally and providing educational psychology as appropriate).[12]

The research amply underpins the importance of school for foster children. A number of questions arise:

- Should a wide view be taken of the importance of school, one that emphasises its social as well as its educational importance?

- Is there a need for greater clarity over the relative roles of foster carers and social workers over education, either in general or in relation to particular foster children?

- Should there be training for foster carers which not only emphasises the importance of school but also discusses the practical steps they can take to encourage a foster child at school?

- Is there a need for a closer working relationship between schools, social workers, foster carers and educational psychologists over the education of looked-after children?

- Is there a need to build on the educational gains after the child has left the placement through greater efforts to enable him or her to get and maintain appropriate jobs?

Chapter 10

Recruitment and Retention

You don't do it for money but you can't afford to do it without the money. (Carer)

If they were only doing it for the money and they hadn't got that sort of special something, they wouldn't be able to do the job. (Social worker)

Introduction

If foster care is to survive and flourish enough carers have to be recruited and enough of them have to stay. Stress in these carers is certainly associated with poorer outcomes[3,11] and arguably helps to cause them.[3] Irrespective of its possible effect on outcomes there is a moral case for providing support. Foster carers put themselves and their families 'on the line'. Generally they find caring highly rewarding – few, probably around 10 per cent of those there at the beginning of the year, have left by the end of it.[10,15] Nevertheless, foster care can have a devastating effect on carers exposed, for example, to allegations of abuse or facing a traumatic placement breakdown. Support is needed to promote recruitment, enable retention and reduce stress, and also as a matter of morality.

Recruitment

One key to increasing the number of foster carers is to increase the number recruited. The experience of the independent sector and of schemes dependent on minority ethnic carers suggests that this is possible. Some authorities had proved able to recruit high proportions of carers from the ethnic minority population.[10] Their success in doing this should have lessons for authorities which have been less successful. What have the core studies themselves to say about recruitment?

Only one study[15] deals in detail with recruitment. The researchers were critical of the methods used. These mainly involved *ad hoc* campaigns whose frequency was constrained by lack of experienced staff and finance. Generally the campaigns emphasised local need, the fact that 'anybody could foster', the demands of the job and the availability of support. There was less evidence that they were targeted at particular groups (e.g. care workers), or that they stressed positive financial rewards or the possibility of future qualifications. They tended to promote a rather 'undifferentiated' view of fostering, or one that emphasised its long-term aspects. A more differentiated approach would need to take account of the common and differing motives of carers, and of the common and different roles they play.

The level of remuneration is probably one key element in recruitment. Most foster carers are not well off. In Kirton et al.'s study four in ten carer families reported an income under £10,000 and only one in five an income of £25,000 or more.[5] So income is important for some potential carers and at least necessary for most.[1,5,10] Those recently recruited seem to attribute more importance to it than older foster carers.[5] So too did those who had a 'professional orientation' and who regarded the fee as an alternative to an income from work outside the home.[5]

Despite these financial considerations, altruism, albeit qualified by finance,[5] is the main reason for fostering[1,13] and a liking for children a necessary condition. Others foster for different reasons – for example to create a family, to compensate for children who have left or, in contrast, because of a desire for a challenge.[13] The latter may respond to an advertisement asking for carers for special schemes for adolescents. They may fail to respond to advertisements suggesting a need to provide long-term foster care for young children. Carers also have different needs. As discussed later in this chapter, carers consider fostering in the context of their family situation. This fact has to be kept in mind in presenting foster care as well as in supporting it. For example, to recruit or maintain more foster carers who need or want to take paid work outside the home it may be necessary to look at providing out-of-school activities and holiday provision. Some of these carers may be attracted by salaried or professional schemes of foster care.

At present lone carers and female carers with outside paid work are less frequent in the population than would be expected among families caring for children.[10] If they are to be recruited their particular needs have to be considered. Married couples with large houses and religious affiliations are probably more common among foster carers than in the general population.[15] So too are carers in 'personal service' occupations. Campaigns should not neglect this group.

It is also important to consider why more people are not attracted to fostering. Carers themselves[15] put forward the following reasons:

- a lack of awareness of the need for fostering

- a fear of not measuring up to agency expectations

- a lack of confidence in their ability to parent someone else's child

- the poor image of foster children

- distrust of social workers and of their ability to tell the truth about fostering or deliver promised services.

These findings help to define the messages that recruitment has to convey – for example, about the need for carers, the support provided by agencies and the joy that foster children can bring. It may also have implications for the way the message is conveyed – for example, through the use of experienced carers who may be trusted or foster children who can help dispel stereotypes.

In practice messages about foster care reach potential carers in different ways. Triseliotis et al.[15] found that around two in every five carers learnt about fostering by word of mouth – that is, from friends, relatives and through contacts at work. A similar proportion responded to feature articles and advertisements mainly in the local press or to TV documentaries. Less common were approaches related to particular children. These related to only 3 per cent of carers and the researchers felt they could be used more often. Carers themselves suggested more use of networks of foster carers to increase recruitment and of foster children to 'sell foster care'.

A good message needs to be complemented by an efficient system. In the Scottish study 80 per cent of enquiries did not result in an application.[15] Four out of ten of those applying did not become carers.[15] English local authorities also reported large, if varying, drop out between application and acceptance.[5] Response at the enquiry and application phase is therefore crucial. Triseliotis et al.[15] found that those joining wanted promptness, efficiency and a knowledgeable and sympathetic follow-up. There should be a chance to meet an experienced carer and attend an open meeting. Generally foster carers felt that the preparation period was too long and that four months was adequate. Staff in the authorities felt that six months was realistic.

This Scottish research suggested that successful recruitment would be based on:

- good knowledge of the area and fostering needs
- a positive image of foster care in the local area
- close work with experienced carers
- a well-organised system for responding to enquiries and following up with a visit if needed
- ensuring involvement of social workers and managers
- use of local media
- steady and consistent promotion.

In practice the research suggested that recruitment was too often haphazard, inadequately targeted and unable to convey a positive but realistic image of fostering. The researchers recommended that:

- Long-term strategies for recruitment should be developed involving the whole agency, informed by local knowledge, using local media, and backed by an efficient system for responding to enquiries.

- Experienced carers and young people who have experienced fostering should be involved at all stages to give a true picture of the work and address misconceptions held about fostering.

- Neighbouring authorities should work together on recruitment to spread cost and avoid duplication.

Recruitment and support of relative carers

The research has rather little to say on the crucial issue of the recruitment of relative carers. Hunt[4] suggests that these carers are more likely to be recruited if they are involved from the beginning, for example through family group conferences or by being made party to legal proceedings. Farmer and Moyers[17] found that most relative or friend placements were initiated by the relatives or friends themselves (86%) and very few by social workers (4%). Some relatives did not become involved because they did not know that the child was in the care system. There may therefore be more scope to involve relatives as carers if social workers are more proactive. Differing practice in these matters may help explain the wide differences between authorities in the use of relative carers.

Hunt[4] also suggests that more thought needs to be paid to policy relating to relative carers. Certainly these carers have some particular needs. As already pointed out they tend to be poorer and in less good health than other carers, many of them do not think of themselves as carers and although they quite commonly become involved in family disputes about caring for their relative, contact is rarely supervised by a social worker. Hunt suggests that they probably need a system of support that differs from that given to other carers. Very probably she is right. At a minimum they need access to the levels of support available for ordinary unrelated foster carers.

Stress, support and ceasing to foster

Any discussion of the strains of foster care needs first to acknowledge its satisfactions. In the core studies the great majority found caring fulfilling[10] and were satisfied with their placements.[3] The turnover among carers was low – no more than 10 per cent of carers left in a year.[5,10,15] This was partly because of their awareness of the need for carers,[15] their commitment to individual children[10,15] and their delight in these children's progress.[10,15] Judged by standard tests the 'mental health' of carers was not poor,[3,10] although it may have suffered in particular respects.[3] Inevitably, some were under strain but this is not necessarily to do with foster care.[10] Their health, as they reported it, seemed at least comparable with that of other people in their age group.[5]

Nevertheless there are strains in fostering. Some of these stem from the nature of the job: the comings and goings of children, sadness at the departure of former foster children, children's behaviour, placement breakdowns, allegations and the need to work closely with parents.[1,10,15] Others relate to the organisation and culture of departments. These include considerable dissatisfaction with the fairness, level and nature of pay and allowances; organisational inefficiency; and a widespread feeling that carers are neither adequately valued nor treated as professional members of a team.[3,5,10,15] Others relate to the private lives of the carers – bereavements or marital difficulties that may or may not have to do with foster care.

Unsurprisingly the carers of adolescents[3] reported particular feelings of strain. At the first interview 81 per cent of carers reported difficulties in 'social functioning'. This meant that they did not feel able to carry out their activities decisively, successfully and within a reasonable time. Almost all (98%) carers reported these problems at second interview. Nearly half the carers confessed to background worries about allegations. Strained carers were less likely to report support from friends or frequent visits from a social worker. They were more likely to report behaviour problems and violence in the foster children.

The pressures on carers to give up are balanced by their strong commitment to individual foster children. In two large studies about 50 per cent of current carers had thought at least occasionally of ceasing to foster.[10,15] Carers thinking of ceasing were commonly aware of the need for carers and committed to individual children.[15] They were unlikely to leave until the child they were currently fostering moved on.[10]

Statistical and qualitative data suggested that carers actually ceased caring for four main reasons – because they did not see fostering as fitting in with their lives (e.g. their age, family situation, need to take paid work outside the home),[10,15] because they were ill supported,[10,15] because of the impact of caring on their families[10,15] or because of distressing events (notably disruptions, allegations, difficulties with birth families and difficulties involving their family).[10]

This analysis suggests that satisfaction with fostering, strains and decisions over continuing all relate to:

- the carer's general family situation
- the quality of support or lack of it
- events in foster care (e.g. breakdowns).

We argue below that support similarly needs to be tailored to the carer's situation and to be high quality and responsive to events and particular difficulties.

Tailoring support to the carer's situation

Carers had varying aspirations and varying sources of help available to them. Some female carers wanted or needed to take paid work outside the home, some did not. Some lived with partners and children, others were on their own. Formal support may need to be adapted to these different situations and in particular to the needs of carers who are: on their own, want to work or are working outside the home, are relative carers and are older than others.

Lone carers were particularly dependent on friends and other support outside the family.[3,10] Such support was related to whether they continued to foster[10] whereas there was no such association in other groups. Such carers may find it difficult to attend training[3] or to manage emergencies such as temporary illness. They need support that can respond to these difficulties (e.g. through enabling a relative of the carer to take the child in emergency).

Some *working carers* reported strain in combining foster care and paid work outside the home.[10] Carers working outside the home were less likely to attend training.[5,10] Some carers said that they were thinking of leaving to take outside work.[10] In keeping with this, former foster carers[15] and inactive foster carers[10] were both more likely to be working outside the home than active ones. Solutions to the problem of combining outside paid work and foster care would involve either enabling outside work (e.g. through after-school care) or defining foster care more clearly as 'work' – something which provides money, status, a pension, a sense of playing a valuable role in a common endeavour and career progression. In the remuneration study around six out of ten carers wanted a salary which would be payable throughout the year.

Relative carers were more socially disadvantaged than other carers with worse housing and lower levels of education. Despite these problems they received on average less remuneration, much less training and preparation and less social work support. In other respects they were a far from homogeneous group. They included grandmothers, aunts and other relatives. Some felt that as relatives they were not by definition foster carers. Such carers did not necessarily want training or support and might see social work as intrusive. Others did see themselves as carers and resented what they saw as the greater support available to others. Quarrels with family members were extremely common, reflecting either pre-existing family difficulties or disputes over who should care for that particular child.[4,10,17]

These problems suggest that relative carers may need a rather different kind of support. Some issues are particular to them. For example, those who do not define themselves as foster carers may not want to join carer groups. These differences do not suggest that they are less likely to need support. They too may take children who are reacting to recent traumas and they do so not as a considered choice of life-style but out of a sense of family obligation.[17] So they need attention to their practical problems, and opportunities for individual support from social workers and other professionals, to meet with others in similar situations, and to take part in training related to their foster children's needs.

Older carers are another significant group. The most recent study[5] emphasised the need to consider the role of older carers. It found that 20 per cent of female carers and 25 per cent of male carers were over the age of 55. This is a rather older profile than given by earlier studies, which had suggested that carers other than those involved in shared care fostering were predominantly aged between 40 and 55 and had fostered for around seven years.[10,15]

Carers over the age of 55 were significantly more likely to cease fostering, defining themselves as 'retiring' although still in some cases willing to provide other services to foster care.[10] Unless these carers can be replaced or, to some extent, redeployed, the effect of their loss on the experience and numbers in the workforce could be serious. In practice there may be a chance to use their invaluable experience in, for example, training, recruitment, fostering panels or short-break fostering. In this way carers' involvement in fostering would be tailored to the way they see their lives. Some of the carers' demands for additional carer involvement in planning, training and preparation might also be met.

Providing high quality support

Carers' attitudes towards caring and the strain they felt reflected the combination of formal and informal support they reported.[10] Children and spouses were key sources of support. Social services cannot, however, guarantee such support although they can seek to acknowledge and encourage it. A key method of doing this is through the formal support they themselves provide. Interestingly, one study[3] suggested that carers who felt that they had good formal support also reported good informal support. Another, similarly, found that carers who felt well supported were less likely to see the children as being more difficult than expected, to want respite, to say that their expectations had not been met or to say that they commonly thought of giving up fostering.[15]

All the studies that consider formal support in any detail provide a similar picture. Carers want respect; efficiency; reliable, warm support from social workers; good information on foster children; responsive out-of-hours services; relief breaks when they need them; information on entitlements; fair remuneration (better pay and conditions); appropriate training and an absence of avoidable hassles (e.g. quarrels over insurance when a foster child damages their house or delays in responding to a young person's request). Some also have more particular points to make; for example, about the handling of allegations, respite and out-of-hours emergencies. These requirements depend on culture (e.g. in the practice of demonstrating respect) and provision (e.g. respite care).[5,10,15]

Support, as various core studies point out, is a 'package deal' in which all aspects including pay have to be appropriate.[3,10,15] Remuneration, for example, is seldom, if ever, the sole reason for fostering.[5] Similarly it is not enough on its own.[5] Indeed, one study found that higher remuneration was associated with above average strain, presumably because it was associated with young people with greater difficulties.[10] Nevertheless, remuneration is important. Each requirement, however, raises particular issues of its own.

Finance

In all the relevant studies all but a small minority of carers (around one in seven) felt that fostering was a job and should be paid appropriately.[5,10,15] Generally they pointed to low incomes, lack of pensions and lack of income in breaks between fostering. They also complained about inequity and lack of clarity over entitlements, difficulties in claiming one-off grants and inefficiency in providing information over entitlements and responding to claims.[5,10,15] This situation reflected the plethora of different schemes and ways of payment, the lack of clarity over grants and insurance, the lack of recognition given to some costs (e.g. those incurred by babies or at the beginning of a fostering career). In some cases it may also have reflected social work or finance department inefficiency over paperwork.[3,5,10,15] One study found that the level of remuneration and allowance was associated with continuing to foster.[10] These issues are clearly key in any programme designed to recruit and keep more foster carers.

Training and preparation

The key issues in training concern its content and effectiveness. These we consider briefly at the end of this chapter. In addition, however, training acts as a form of support. It puts carers in touch with other foster carers from whom they can seek support and advice.[5,10] One study[10] suggested that above-average hours of training was associated with experiencing greater support from other carers and with above-average levels of remuneration. This combination was associated with a greater likelihood that the carer would continue to foster. Arguably, such carers were more likely to feel that they were part of a profession, something that commanded at least some salary and had a sense of identity. In general the level of training was quite low,[10] with the highest level reported an average of 25 hours' training per carer in the 12 months prior to interview.[3] All the relevant studies suggested that carers valued the training they received and found it relevant.[5,10,15] However, they did want more training and more involvement from other carers in providing it. In addition there were problems over timing and venue. As already discussed, certain groups found it particularly difficult to attend. These included carers under 40 (probably because of childcare difficulties),[15] lone carers[3] and carers working outside the home.[5,10] In addition one study[5] reported that experienced carers often found training repetitive and insufficiently challenging. Relative carers had very little training indeed, although in some, but not all, cases this may have reflected choice.

Carer groups

Many carers value carer groups.[5,10] Like training, they put carers in touch with other carers and perhaps foster a sense of professional identity. The problems of attendance partly reflect the practical problems that affect training, partly choice (groups are not everyone's 'cup of tea') and partly availability. They can be difficult to organise in rural areas where long distances are involved. In general, the studies would suggest that they should, ideally, be available but not mandatory for all. Where distance makes this impractical, alternative methods (for example, Internet groups) may be needed. In addition some authorities seemed to build on the willingness of carers to seek support from each other by promoting individual links between one carer and another.

Social work support

All the relevant studies suggest that carers want social workers who are available, responsive and able to listen, who treat the carer as a partner and do not patronise, who give honest information, and who understand foster care and the needs of foster carers' families. Such attributes are built on availability, a willingness to respond quickly and, at the minimum, returned telephone calls. The carers in Triseliotis *et al.*'s study[15] wanted more visits from social workers. In the first York study[10] carers who were less frequently visited by link or fostering social workers (now known as supervising social workers or SSWs) were more likely to cease fostering. (Interestingly, telephone contact was equally associated with continuing[10] and was also used in independent fostering agencies (IFAs) to supplement face-to-face contact.[5]) Kirton *et al.*[5] also found that the reported frequency and length of SSW contacts were both strongly associated with the carer's sense of being supported.

All the relevant studies agree that foster carers valued link or fostering social workers more highly than the child's social worker and particularly so if they worked from specialised teams.[15] One study[3] reported that carers valued the feeling that they had a team behind them – not just one worker who might not be available when needed. However, there are also other reasons. Social workers know less about foster care. They are commonly preoccupied with emergencies and the priorities of childcare – their failure to respond to telephone calls is a major complaint. There is also a conflict of roles. In the end it is the job of the social worker to support the child and not the carer. The potential conflict may be exacerbated when things start to go wrong.

To avoid such conflicts completely might be collusive. Nevertheless it should be possible to reduce their frequency and harmfulness. Common training, placements as part of training in teams of link workers and creative use of the existence of both link workers and social workers to make conflict constructive might all help. So too might greater awareness of the importance of making foster carers feel supported by a team when a child's social worker is not available. Annoyance might be reduced by a greater delegation to carers so that they no longer need to seek permission for, say, sleepovers and impatiently wait for a response. A failure to return telephone calls should probably not be acceptable at all.

Night duty teams

Out-of-hours services were important to some carers and varied widely in quality.[3,5,10] Common complaints were that the teams were not well informed about foster care and were less concerned with solving problems than with 'passing the buck' to their colleagues on the next working day.[3,11] Carers in the adolescent fostering study and in Triseliotis *et al.*'s study emphasised the need for specialised out-of-hours emergency response teams, although these might in some cases be under-used.[5]

Short breaks

Attitudes to breaks varied – some wanted them, some did not, and some were reluctant to take them if they could not leave the child at home with someone they knew. Undoubtedly many carers wanted them strongly and carers in the Scottish special scheme considered them essential.[16] Researchers asking groups of carers to make recommendations noted requests for more respite[5,15] and related provisions such as sitting schemes or out-of-school provision.[5] They also noted complaints that short breaks were only available if the carer had to 'beg' or that, while these breaks were theoretically available as part of a support package, they were not provided in practice.[9,10] The studies did not provide evidence of the impact of these breaks but it seems likely that they should be more widely available. Their use and usefulness might also be enhanced if arrangements were made for ensuring that the same child went to the same carer for a break. One way of doing this might be to register relatives of the carer to provide these breaks. Another might involve creating groups of carers who were able to take each other's children.

Preparation for placements

It was very important to carers that the children placed with them fitted their household and that they knew enough about them in advance to prepare for any difficulties. As already discussed there was some evidence that lack of information was both common and associated with placement breakdown.[3,11] In contrast, carers who were given written care plans were more satisfied.[5] Similarly, carers who were looking after children who did not fit their preferences as to gender were in one study more likely to experience a placement breakdown.[3] In another study[10] carers were asked about the kind of children they preferred to take or avoid. Those who had experience of their preferences being ignored had rather more negative attitudes towards fostering. Neglect of their preferences hardly reflects the respect and teamwork to which they aspired.

Teamwork

Carers described their rapport with agencies as poor, despite generally good personal relationships with individual staff.[15] Few examples were given of teamwork or shared planning between staff and carers. This was important to carers.[3,5,10] Those who experienced a lack of teamwork and respect were aggrieved. Better teamwork and better sharing of information were part of the shopping list put forward by the carers in Triseliotis *et al.*'s study.[15] Those who felt valued as a colleague were much more likely to feel well supported[5] while, conversely, those who did not feel that their views were taken seriously were much more likely to feel under strain.[3]

Dealing with events

The extent of strain on foster carers varied over time. One study[10] developed a list of events that were expected to be particularly stressful. These included allegations, placement breakdowns, contact with very difficult parents and disruption to the family attributed to the foster child. Carers who had experienced such problems had significantly worse mental health.

Allegations were an occupational hazard. In one study 16 per cent of current carers reported having experienced one.[10] Triseliotis *et al.*'s study[15] suggested that 3.5 per cent of carers are subject to an allegation every year. However, out of 78 carers who were accused only 12 were deregistered. This suggests that over an average foster care 'lifetime' of seven years a carer should have around a one in five chance of being subject to an allegation.

Despite the rarity of proven allegations anxiety about them was a background worry to many carers.[3] Quite often it led to considerable constrictions in lifestyle so that, for example, arrangements were made to ensure that carers were not in the same car as a female foster child without an escort. The effect of allegations once made could be devastating. Carers commonly appreciated that the charges had to be taken seriously. They resented, however, the sense that they were cut off from support. Sometimes they did not know the result of the investigations that were made, and were left, as it were, in limbo with nothing resolved. Over a third of carers in the study of adolescents either had no knowledge of procedures for handling allegations (15%) or were dissatisfied with what they knew (21%).[3]

Breakdowns were painful. They greatly enhanced the likelihood that a carer would leave since they often simultaneously increased motivation to do so and removed the felt obligation to look after a particular foster child.[10] Despite this there seemed to be no widespread policy that ensured that these events were treated seriously and sympathetically or that any necessary lessons were learnt.

Contacts with birth family could also be difficult. At an abstract level carers were generally in favour of contact but they were more likely to mention it as a cause of stress.[15] As already discussed, difficulties included the effect on the child of parents' failures to visit as promised, or even abuse; the impact on the carer/child relationship with the parent; setting the child against the carer, and drunkenness and aggression directed at carer.[10,11,12,15] The most common method of managing such contacts seemed to be to change the venue.[15] This might be expected to be a reasonably effective, if not necessarily constructive, solution.

The *impact of fostering on the carer's family* was a further area of difficulty. It was obvious from particular cases that foster care can exacerbate strains in a marriage. Fifteen per cent of the adolescents' foster carers said that the young person's placement had had a negative impact on their relationship with their partner, while another 15 per cent reported a positive effect.[3] This, however, seems to have been too delicate an area for most of the core studies to explore. They were more forthright in their explorations of the impact on the carers' children. As already discussed, the impact of fostering on birth children seemed to be one of the ways in which difficulties in the placement led to breakdown. Despite the importance of this issue, the studies recorded little systematic good practice in tackling it.

Conclusion

An increase in the number of carers requires an increase in the number recruited. Turnover should also not increase or should, if possible, be reduced. Support is needed to achieve these ends and should reduce turnover. It should also increase recruitment as foster carers advertise their good experience by word of mouth.

There is evidence that this should be possible. In one study[5] the proportion of carers who felt well supported varied from 28 per cent to 63 per cent in 16 local authorities and 67 per cent to 88 per cent in 5 IFAs. This may not represent an inherent superiority or lasting advantage for the independent sector. The sample of IFAs was not random. Those who agreed to take part in the research may have been particularly successful. In addition, the apparent superiority of the IFAs may have rested on their higher salaries, better staffing ratios of SSWs and other factors that could be replicated if local authorities had adequate funding. What it strongly suggests is that authorities can affect perceptions of support.

A second key piece of evidence comes from the Scottish study of treatment foster care.[16] Some at least of the young people who entered the programme would otherwise have been in secure provision. Despite this none of the 28 carers recruited to the programme left over the period of its operation. This low turnover was a tribute to the principles on which the programme was based – parity of respect for carers and social workers, payment for carers based on a scale for residential workers, a dedicated out-of-hours service, close support from social workers and carer groups, and eight weeks of breaks per year from caring. The scheme also succeeded in attracting new carers who had not previously fostered. It is, as it were, an experimental demonstration of the basic requirements for foster care support.

The challenge for local authorities is therefore to 'catch up with' the performance of some independent fostering agencies. In doing this they will need to consider:

- Improving the levels and continuity of reward for foster carers. Most want a salary and a pension.

- Conveying positive but realistic messages about fostering to the general public, involving carers and foster children in this task, targeting their recruitment to specific groups, and responding positively and efficiently to enquiries.

- Improving the efficiency with which payments are made, costs for transport and damage reimbursed, and financial requests considered. This may be enhanced by a combination of inviting carers to submit certain claims direct to finance via email; allowing for general wear and tear through general grant; and devolving budgets for some exceptional expenditure to SSWs, thus enabling prompt decision.[5]

- Dedicated out-of-hours teams in authorities large enough to justify them or specialist out-of-hours work provided by a rota of SSWs.

- Training programmes with a logical progression which are delivered at 'carer-friendly' hours, in pleasant surroundings and which are supported by payments for transport and childcare.

- Using the expertise of experienced carers who no longer wish to foster full time, perhaps by providing them with roles in training, publicity or relief care.

- Carer groups which are supported by similar provision and which may include specialised groups (e.g. for 'children who foster').
(Internet-based smart groups and chat rooms might be alternatives for those not able to attend the groups.)

- Respite care made available to those who request it on an agreed basis combined with an opportunity to place children with known carers.

- Out-of-school provision that may similarly support carers who work outside the home.

- Preparation for placements which takes into account carer preferences and includes written information on care plans.

- Regular contact with SSWs at least once a month and preferably more frequently, that should probably be supplemented by regular telephone contact.

- A prompt response to events in general and breakdowns in particular.

- A protocol for responding to allegations which includes the provision of independent support to the carer.

- Training which prepares carers for the emotional impact of their job, the pain of losing foster children and the challenging behaviour they may encounter.

There is evidence that support for foster carers is most effective if it is tailored to their particular family situation; combines regular social work visits with relevant training, contact with other carers in training or groups and adequate remuneration; pays attention to the particular issues raised by carers such as the need for a good after-hours service; is responsive to 'events'; and makes carers feel they are part of a team. Questions that arise include:

- Is support responsive to the needs of particular families, taking into account the motivation and competencies of carers, the contribution of children, the role of the wider family, the strength of their informal support network, and the particular difficulties of lone carers and carers who work outside the home?

- Is the basic level of support – including finance, training and social work contact – adequate to the needs of carers and comparable across the independent and local authority sectors?

- Do social workers develop a working relationship with the carers, including them in planning, keeping appointments and responding to telephone calls? Do all relevant policies and procedures emphasise the need to involve carers?

- Do the procedures for responding to allegations and breakdowns emphasise the need to attend to the emotional needs of the carers as well as those of the child?

Chapter 11

Training, Professional Support and Organisation

Introduction

We have looked at the key actors in foster care and the recruitment and retention of foster carers themselves. Our penultimate chapter looks at four issues which provide the back-up for foster care: training, support from social workers, support from other professionals, and organisation.

Training

Initial preparation for fostering was usually done in groups and was generally found to be helpful. As we have seen subsequent training was also praised. Despite these good opinions Triseliotis *et al.*[15] were critical of the way training often seemed to be provided, seeing its provision as spasmodic and lacking in any clear plan. They provided a list of areas that in their view ought to be covered. These were:

- the role of foster care, its location in department, its legal context, rights and expectations of those involved
- relevant theory – attachment, child development, abuse
- routine care (hygiene, safety in home, etc.).

Key professional issues included:

- the emotional impact of fostering on carers
- the handling of difficult behaviour, including problems relating to sexual abuse, drugs and alcohol
- contact with parents, 'letting children go'
- key practical issues – including those relating to finance and allegation procedures.

In addition they argued that preparation before fostering should be seen as training and linked to subsequent training and, if wanted, to a qualification.

These authors do not consider how training should be provided or what subsequent support might be needed. By contrast Macdonald and Kakavelakis[6] provide a detailed description of training based on social learning and including considerable practice. Their experiment did not 'work'. The reasons for this were unclear. They could have included the inappropriateness of the theory, the way it was interpreted, the lack of intensity in the training or failures in the way the training was applied and taken up.

What is important is the demonstration that training, however logical, does not always result in an improvement in performance. We do not know what is necessary for this to happen. Arguably training needs to be part of a coherent system. Social workers and link workers need to be working according to the same theory. This was certainly true of the successful US treatment foster care programme.[23] It is, however, unclear whether this was the key to the programme's success.

In advance of this knowledge the present studies include numerous findings and insights that could well be incorporated into training. These include issues related to contacts, the handling of attachment and difficult behaviour, school, identity, and the need for carers to respond to a child's emotional age, to encourage children to develop skills appropriate to their age and to monitor an adolescent's activities outside the home. At present we know quite a lot about the practice of successful carers. We know rather less about how to teach it. This, however, should not prevent efforts to do so.

Support from social workers

All the stages of foster care involve social workers. They are key players in the decision that a child should or should not be looked after. They orchestrate the placement process. Once the child is placed they support carers; intervene when relationships between carer and child become difficult; have a key role in enabling, mediating or forbidding contact; help decide whether or not a child should return home or be adopted; and arrange support both during the placement process and after. Implicitly, therefore, all the discussion and recommendations in this report involve them.

General points about social work practice are implicit in these discussions of particular aspects of practice. The reports bring out the need for social workers to be aware of their perceived power. Parents wanting short-term 'respite', adoptive parents wanting moral support or receiving assessment and parents looking after a returned child all face a dilemma.[1,12] They often want help, they are aware that to get this help they have to expose a problem, conscious that too serious a revelation may result in consequences such as the loss of their child, and uncertain of the rules by which this game is played. In confronting this dilemma parents, adoptive parents, the foster children and the foster carers have certain common requirements of social workers. They want workers who listen; understand their position; are warm; are prompt, practical and efficient; are straight – not saying one thing and doing another – and are reliable, answering telephone calls and coming when they say they will.

The way these qualities are expressed obviously vary with the situation. Foster children value signs that the worker is committed to them beyond the call of duty – perhaps writing after they are no longer officially involved.[13] Living as they do in someone else's house their position is inherently insecure, so it is particularly important that the social worker listens to them and promotes what they want. Children value workers who are active in getting them the kind of contact they want with relatives, in supporting their particular hobbies, or in moving them from places they find intolerable.[11,12] Foster carers object to social workers who appear to be always sick or on leave, or who do not sort out the paperwork as this has practical consequences for them. Parents object to social workers who judge them without understanding. Potential adopters object to delay and to assessments that seem indirect, opaque or unfair.[12]

Social workers can only respond to these expectations if they have a clear remit. If they lack autonomy or are uncertain of the rules under which they operate they cannot give their clients the speedy, clear response they crave. The core studies did not describe how far social workers felt themselves to be organisational ciphers. They did, however, suggest that it is often difficult to give them clear rules. Principles conflicted and exceptions abounded. It was highly desirable to place children in ethnically matched placements. Sometimes this would mean moving them from placements in which they were settled. It was important to keep siblings together. Sometimes, however, this would overwhelm the placement or lead to long delay.[8] Such situations require careful professional assessments. Social workers need to be skilled and empowered to make them.

Other professionals

Both social workers and carers feel that foster children receive insufficient psychological help. They also tend to feel that the help that is provided is often too little and too late. Child and adolescent mental health services were particularly criticised for failing to respond until the foster child was in a stable situation.[5,9]

One study[11] documented the range of outside professionals involved with foster care. The list included psychiatrists, counsellors, different kinds of psychologists and speech therapists. Statistics on the outcomes of their help were not encouraging. 'Behavioural help' was associated with a reduction in difficult behaviours such as violence in one study.[11] It did not, however, appear to affect overall success. With the important exception of educational psychology, contact with any form of professional was associated with failure, sometimes significantly so.[11]

Two studies did provide more encouraging results. One[3] reported that counselling was associated with successful placements and 'appropriate psychological help' with the avoidance of breakdown. Another found that educational psychology was associated with both success and the avoidance of breakdown.[11] The relevant studies suggested that both counselling and educational psychology were provided to more difficult young people. It is unlikely therefore that the characteristics of the young people explain the results. It is possible, however, that these services are most likely to be provided in circumstances where the placement is stable and the young person and carer are both keen to tackle issues not directly related to it. Further research is needed to determine whether this explains the results.

Overall the studies do not cast doubt on the hypothesis that professional intervention could have a good effect. Some children were very grateful for the help provided.[12] Some carers were similarly positive.[9] Others might benefit if there was a closer alliance between those providing psychological help and the carers so that children could discuss their feelings in both settings.[18] However, the studies do not suggest that the current intensity or quality of these services is such as to routinely affect outcomes for good.

Organisational structure and practice

Triseliotis et al.[15] provide a detailed description of organisation in Scottish authorities and they make some comparisons with England. They describe a system which in their view often lacked a strong policy framework, direction and political commitment. The profile of the fostering service was generally low and swamped by concerns with child protection. Developments were constrained by a lack of resources and dependent on the interests of particular managers or councillors, and on working groups. Other studies[1,14,16] document the important but fragile role of special projects in pioneering high quality service.

Triseliotis et al. discuss the advantages and disadvantages of the varied organisational arrangements they describe. Specialist fostering services, albeit sometimes joined with adoption or other services, were not closely integrated with fieldwork. They were seen as acquiring expertise, fostering development, allowing an accessible point of contact and providing an overview. Joint teams were seen as avoiding unhealthy identification by social workers with foster carers and promoting cooperation rather than conflict between different kinds of social worker. Some functions (panel approvals, carer review, advertising and recruitment) were generally organised as specialist functions.

There was widespread use of external provision usually purchased on a 'spot' basis. The existence of these external or specialist services implied mechanisms for authorising their funding and controlling their quality. Some authorities were moving towards purchaser/provider splits, whereby services could be purchased internally or externally. This was promoted as leading to clearer aims and the development of higher quality provision. It could be attacked as splitting off managers from the frontline knowledge of providers, as raising costs by moving them towards market rates, and for endangering communication between professionals.

Quality assurance mechanisms included written standards, manuals for carers, fostering panels, recording breakdown rates (only a quarter of the authorities did this), reviews, systematic feedback from carers, written allegation procedures, and the involvement of foster carers. Very little use was made of data routinely collected for management purposes to access vacancies; record the characteristics of those waiting; match carer and child; monitor recruitment, loss of carers, outcome of placements, disruption rates or the ethnicity of carers; or provide a profile of children needing placement. The contribution of carers and foster children was largely unsystematic.

A key feature of the organisations described by Triseliotis *et al.*[15] was the amount of change. Less than half of them (40%) said they had reached organisational stability. A quarter were reorganising themselves and a further two fifths thinking of doing so. This belief in the potential of structural change seemed to have little foundation in the research. As illustrated above, most forms of organisation had something to be said for them and something to be said against them. There was no strong evidence that they had an impact on quality of care. For example, there were very large organisational differences between the authorities in the York studies.[10,11,12] There were also differences in efficiency as perceived by carers. There were no significant differences in the rate of placement breakdown, which seemed to be determined at the level of foster carer and child rather than by the structural context in which they met.

Conclusion

Consistent, coherent training is hard to supply in foster care and when supplied is not necessarily supported after it has taken place. Training seems to influence carer morale but there is a lack of evidence that it influences outcomes. Methods of training need to be developed, tried out and rigorously evaluated until successful ones are found.

In this context a number of suggestions can be made:

- Key people at a senior level within the organisation should have responsibility for promoting training programmes and ensuring the arrangements are adhered to.

- Skills training should be of sufficient length, breadth and depth to allow skills to be acquired.

- Trainers should consider explicit contractual arrangements about attendance and practice between sessions supported by social workers and managers.

- There should be incentives for completing training in the form of cash or NVQs or the offer of using the skills acquired in further training.

- Participants who find difficulty in grasping the concepts may require individual attention.

- The training requires follow-up, perhaps 'problem clinics' to which carers experiencing difficulties may drop in, and link workers who have been trained alongside carers in the method and are able to observe and support its practice.

- Training packages should focus on what works in terms of realistic preparation. There should be additional ongoing training in handling stressful placements.

- There should be joint training of carers with social workers, which would improve working relationships and promote understanding of roles.

The core studies did not make organisation their primary focus. Conclusions drawn from them therefore have to be tentative. On balance, they suggest the need for a strong policy framework that has political endorsement and ensures:

- adequate resources

- efficient management of central procedures (e.g. over the reimbursement of foster carers)

- high standard central resources (e.g. specialised night duty teams for foster care)

- quality assurance which routinely adopts best practice (e.g. involvement of carers and foster children)

- efficient use of information systems both to monitor the system and for operational purposes

- a programme of development which harnesses the enthusiasm of particular individuals or groups and ensures new approaches (e.g. shared care or treatment foster care) are tried out on a pilot basis and then rolled out more widely.

There is at present no evidence that any particular organisational structure is, on balance, better than another.

There is a lack of evidence on the form of organisation that is likely to promote good foster care. Despite this lack reorganisation is frequent and costly. Evidence on the effectiveness of training is similarly lacking. Questions which arise include:

- Should there be a major focus on developing, evaluating and then disseminating methods of training carers that are effective?
- Should social services concentrate less on structural change and more on creating a culture in which things are done well?

Chapter 12

Conclusion

Introduction

This report has summarised numerous findings. This is not the place to summarise yet further. There may, however, be value in trying to point out the structure of the argument and to highlight some particular points.

The dilemma

Troubled children need relationships with adults who are committed to them. Foster care offers the chance of such relationships. It is a serious response to serious problems. It is valuable and valued.

Despite these advantages foster care faces a dilemma. The children it now shelters have left very difficult situations. Some have continued to live at home to the point where they have lost any chance of adoption. Most do not want to be adopted. Many of those who return home do not appear to do as well as they might have done if they had remained looked after. Those who remain rarely gain a family for life, experiencing instead either placements that break down in adolescence or an expectation that they move on at the age of 18 or earlier. What follows is often difficult and lonely. The key weakness of foster care is thus not so much what happens in foster care but what happens after it.

The principles

The report is built round the need to respond to this dilemma. Our suggestions are grounded in evidence on the needs and wants of foster children. Basically, they want a normal life, a family that accepts them, respect for their origins, an important voice in decisions about them and a springboard to a better life. Most probably need an experience of good parenting, support for developing or maintaining attachments, encouragement to enjoy school and do well there, and support for developing a sense of identity.

A system designed to meet both wishes and needs would in our view:

- promote close relationships
- promote opportunities for the child to grow and change
- pay attention to the child's choice
- offer a coherent connection between what happens in foster care and what happens after it.

These principles should in our view inform all interventions related to foster care. Children are more likely to succeed in foster care if they want to be there, receive skilful, committed parenting, are attached to a trusted adult and have a good experience at school. So social workers and foster carers should operate according to the same understanding of what promotes well-being, provides a sense of identity and inhibits difficult behaviour. These issues are probably equally important when a child returns home. Both parents and foster carers need to understand what kinds of approach may bring these things about.

In following through these principles we have suggested the need for:

- The opportunity for greater support at home, sometimes based on support from former carers or on 'shared care schemes'.

- A greater use of adoption or other measures, such as Special Guardianship, based partly on a greater decisiveness in early assessment and partly on making it easier for carers to adopt.

- A recognition that foster care can enable change, the expansion of treatment foster care and a link between interventions with the child and her or his family (e.g. by training both parents and carers in the same approach).

- The development of a form of foster care that more nearly approaches a 'family for life', which is not seen as 'second best' and in which the carers can act as parents.

The last point is worth elaborating. A significant proportion of children who become looked after will not be able to return to their families, do not want to be adopted and have no realistic possibility of being so. Many of these children want to live with foster carers who act as parental figures and who could offer a life-long relationship. The immediate challenge is to recognise that this is what many children need and to review current policy and practice with the intention of making it possible for more of them. It is also important to ensure that the carers can act as parents, for example, in terms of taking responsibility over authorising school trips.

The principles and different age groups

The above suggestions apply mainly to children who cannot return home and who therefore require adoption or some other form of permanence. Even with this limitation some of the suggestions are likely to be more relevant to children in some age groups than they are to others.

Children who are first looked after when below the age of five have a realistic chance of adoption. Policies designed to promote decisiveness, close monitoring of 'drift', 'parallel planning' and the identification of adoptive placements for 'hard to place groups' are most likely to be relevant to this group.

Children who are first looked after when aged five to ten are much less likely to be adopted. Local authorities may act as 'corporate parents' for some of them over prolonged periods. Policies designed to make their foster families more 'genuinely permanent' (for example, by enabling young people to remain beyond the age of 18) are likely to be particularly relevant to them. Some of this group may also benefit from 'shared care' fostering that seems to have been developed with the needs of this age group in mind.

Children who are first looked after when aged 11 and over are very unlikely to be adopted. Some of them display very difficult behaviour. Few of them will spend very prolonged periods in the care system. Policies that promote treatment foster care, which provide an alternative to residential care or secure provision or which seek to ensure that these young people have a realistic base for independent living, may be particularly relevant to them.

These distinctions by 'age first looked after' may be helpful in forming policy. There are, however, numerous exceptions. Some children enter when aged less than five and for various reasons are looked after long term. Others enter at an older age but are still relatively young. As they grow older they face difficulties in their teens and have placements that break down. They may benefit from some of the approaches in treatment foster care. Some of those who enter as adolescents may require long-term care and a 'family for life'. Needs and age are not therefore related in a particularly close way. What is important is that adequate provision is in place, that the allocation of foster children to different provision is done sensitively and with due regard to the particular features of each situation, and that all provision is of very high quality.

The quality of foster care

In long-term and probably other forms of foster care certain key requirements seem to determine how well the placements go. These requirements relate to:

- the process of making a placement
- the child and her or his needs

- the foster family, particularly the main carer
- contact with the birth family
- the child's school.

In all these areas the research provided evidence that can inform practice and policy. To give some examples, the research provides arguments for a process of placing children that is, as far as possible, more consultative; involves a greater exchange of information and does not match on 'rules of thumb'. It identifies the characteristics of carers associated with good results and the need to prevent 'negative spirals' before bad relationships build up. It underlines the crucial importance of the child's school, and the opportunities carers have for working constructively with child and teachers.

The evidence on contact may be controversial. Contact arrangements are an area of great difficulty and potential conflict. Children generally want to see more of their families although they may also want to see less of particular family members. Contacts themselves are often beneficial but can equally be unsatisfactory and even harmful. The studies suggest that time and effort needs to be spent on making contact a better and safer experience for all concerned. In particular contact with members of the wider family is often overlooked and can often be very helpful.

The needs of carers

The report's suggestions would almost certainly require more foster carers. It therefore considers how more carers can be recruited and how more can be retained as carers. At a basic level this requires that carers are properly valued, remunerated and trained. At the least this would mean that foster carers are paid an allowance that covers the full cost of care and that payment, where received, is based on appropriate comparisons. In addition, there is a need for improved support services for foster carers that give access to 24-hour support, respite care, educational support and tailored support packages that meet the needs of the child and carers. There should also be recognition that allegations, placement breakdowns and other hazards of fostering can have a devastating effect on carers. Appropriate and sensitive responses to these hazards are key elements in effective support.

A particular issue concerns placements with relatives. These have numerous potential advantages. However, relative carers tend to be poorer and worse housed than others. They may be in dispute with the child's family or find it difficult to protect the child from undesirable contacts. The evidence suggests that more children will and can be placed with relatives, but these placements are currently less well supported despite evidence that their needs are at least as great. Local authorities may need to establish specialist support services for relatives who foster so that their needs can be met separately from those of non-relative foster carers.

Organisation

On one issue the evidence is silent. Nothing suggests that organisational change has a beneficial effect. Despite this, change is common. More attention should, perhaps, be paid to the good practice which is certainly needed and on which the research has much more to say. What matters is not so much how foster carers are organised but how they do the job they do.

Conclusion

The report has argued that policy on foster care has to be developed in the context of family support and also adoption. It should aim to promote close relationships, choice, change and coherence between what happens in foster care and what happens after it. It should expand the provision of genuine long-term foster care, but also shared care, treatment foster care and support by carers after a child has ceased to be looked after. It should pay close attention to the key determinants of success in foster care and in particular to the lynchpin of the system: the foster carers themselves.

At the most general level we now know a great deal about how to support foster carers and about the kinds of fostering that foster children need. We know much less about how to produce this fostering. Foster carers who are kind, firm and slow to take offence are likely to have better results than others who embody these antique virtues to a less marked degree. There is much less evidence on how to select, support or train carers so that their performance approximates more closely to this ideal.

Progress will thus depend on two things – on the one hand a willingness to implement the good practice whose nature is already clear and on the other creativity in the development of practice, skill in defining what has been developed and willingness rigorously to evaluate its results. This report is intended to promote the first of these steps and inform the second.

The Researchers' Summaries of their Projects

The following overviews were provided by the researchers and have only been lightly edited. The order follows the numbering system used in the text. The title relates to the main report or publication of the project and not to the name of the study.

Supporting Families through Short-term Fostering[1]

Jane Aldgate and Marie Bradley
School of Health and Social Welfare, The Open University

This study is about a particular kind of family support that local authorities can offer under section 20 of the Children Act 1989. It provides for children to have short-term breaks away from home, defined as no more than four weeks at a time or 90 days over a year with same carer. Such short-term placements have traditionally been offered to families of disabled children but this study investigated their use for other children in need.

Study design

This intensive study of 60 children explored the expectations and outcomes of this particular form of family support from the perspectives of the different parties involved: parents, children, carers, social workers and other professionals. Using a 'before and after' design the researchers traced the progress of 60 children and their families, who were recruited sequentially to the study in four different parts of the country. Parents, children and social workers were interviewed when the service was about to be taken up and then again six to nine months later, or when the arrangement ended if that was sooner. Standardised psychometric tests were administered to parents and children at the start and end of the period to serve as outcome measures, and carers were also interviewed at the second point.

Key findings

- Families using the service were all living in circumstances of considerable stress.
- Parents were very positive about the service and felt it had helped them gain more control over their lives.
- Children had some reservations, but by the end most were reasonably happy with the placement.
- The community basis and voluntary nature of the service helped to make it acceptable to parents.
- More attention needed to be paid to arrangements for ending the service.

- Social workers played a key role in holding the arrangements together.
- For parents with chronic needs, the key to success was the combination of breaks plus other social work support.

THE FAMILIES

The families using the service were all living in circumstances of considerable stress. Most were on very low incomes, with few sources of emotional and practical support and a high incidence of health problems. They were definitely 'in need', but could be divided into those who were facing particular crises but normally coped (acute cases) and those with more on-going, chronic difficulties who were often already known to the social services departments. For the former, short-term accommodation on its own was generally enough to prevent early stresses becoming more serious, but for parents with more chronic needs the key to success was the combination of breaks plus other services, including social work support for themselves and sometimes direct work with the children.

Both groups of parents judged the short-term accommodation service to be a resounding success. They thought it had helped them to address health problems, relationships with partners if they had them, and problems of social isolation. They felt that breaks had given them a chance to build informal support networks, both through re-establishing links with extended family and friends and through developing links in the community via the carers, who mostly lived in their own neighbourhood. Parents described feeling more in control of their lives, and said the breaks had helped them to get things more in perspective. On a more objective level the placements were also shown to work, since only 2 of the 60 failed to prevent family breakdown. Social workers were slightly more cautious in their evaluation than families, but even so they believed their original aims for the placement had been met in practically two thirds of the cases.

THE CHILDREN

The children were more ambivalent in their views. The older ones could appreciate the value of the breaks for their family but were less sure for themselves. Many children worried about what would happen without them at home, about being rejected and not wanted back, and about practical issues like not being able to watch favourite TV programmes or having to eat food they didn't like. Children over the age of five often felt homesick, and coped with this by wanting to be alone – not as a rejection of their carer family, but as a way of coming to terms with their feelings. By the end of the placement, however, most children were more positive about the experience, and with one or two exceptions their needs did not appear to have been subordinated to the needs of their parents.

THE SOCIAL WORKERS

The study also looked at the social work processes that form an essential link between the principles and regulations of the Children Act and successful outcomes for children and families, such as how parents access the service, how social workers consult and work with parents and children, and how the planning and reviewing process is carried out. The findings were broadly positive. Although parents had often found it hard to get information about family support services, two thirds had no difficulty in accepting short-term accommodation for their children once it was offered, partly because many had positive experiences with social services in the past (such as being offered childminding or day care) and so did not perceive social workers in a 'child rescue' role. It was harder for new families without such previous links or for those subject in the past to child protection enquiries, but a model of referral that worked particularly well was when health visitors based within the community and trusted by families were able to refer them directly.

Once families had accepted the service, family support social workers played an important role in holding the arrangements together and managing the placement. The consultation process specified in the guidance and regulations to the Act seemed to be working well. Almost all parents felt they had participated fully in the planning meeting and had helped to shape the childcare plan. Social workers often underestimated the extent to which parents had felt consulted, and the researchers suggest that the concept of partnership needs to be sensitive to different ways of involving parents. Some may be content to be quietly present and consulted; others may need help to rehearse their views prior to the meeting so that they feel confident to express themselves in public.

The one aspect of short-term accommodation arrangements that was unsatisfactory was the way in which they were ended. Too often the carer was left with responsibility for managing the ending of the placement without social work support. When a family had been offered six weekend breaks but was still desperate for support, it was very difficult for carers to say goodbye, and parents had no chance to reflect on what had been achieved. Parents, children and carers all found this a difficult time, and there was a clear need for a more formal and symbolic ending.

What worked?

A number of factors helped to make the short-term accommodation services in the study a success. First, this was a positive service being offered to families on a voluntary basis, which was greatly appreciated. Second, it was a community-based service, which meant that parents and carers lived in the same area, used the same shops and schools, and parents could identify with the carers and see them as role models. They saw the carers as 'like us, but without the problems'. Third, the carers were carefully recruited, often from childminders who were used to offering a service on a business basis to families, and they were reasonably well supported by social workers. Social workers also tended to choose families whom they felt would be able to make good use of short-term breaks, and they were unlikely to offer this particular form of family support to very chaotic or disorganised families who would find it difficult to sustain the arrangement, to families where children were at risk of serious harm, to children with severe behavioural problems, or as a crisis resource. Most important, the input of social workers was crucial in effecting a positive outcome for parents and children. Successful short-term accommodation offered not just relief from stress for harassed parents, but also a social work service that attempted to strengthen families. Social workers worked in partnership with parents, undertook direct work with children and casework with parents, organised and supported the placement, and worked collaboratively with other professionals on behalf of the family.

Messages for policy and practice

This study exemplifies the value of an approach to children's services that focuses on promoting and safeguarding children's welfare. It uses measurable outcomes to show that this kind of short-term fostering, when well targeted, can bring about changes in levels of family problems and help prevent family breakdown. The Quality Protects programme encourages local authorities to develop such provision. The study also underlined the importance of traditional casework and demonstrates how social work is a family support service in its own right, which is valued by parents and children.

Fostering Family Contact: A Study of Children, Parents and Foster Carers[2]

Hedy Cleaver

Department of Health and Social Care, Royal Holloway, University of London

When a local authority looks after children, unless contact orders stipulate otherwise, the Children Act 1989 presumes reasonable contact between separated children and their parents. However, a legal requirement need not necessarily result in a change of practice. This study explores the impact of the Children Act 1989 on contact between foster children and their families.

Study design

The study was set in six local authorities and had two parts: a retrospective survey of 152 social work files to identify whether practice regarding contact had changed since the Children Act; and a qualitative study of 33 foster children aged 5–12 years whom social workers expected to be looked after for at least four months. Interviews with children, key family members, foster carers and social workers were conducted 6 weeks after placement and 12 months later. Outcomes were measured using a number of dimensions, including placement stability, levels of contact and the children's behaviour and well-being.

Key findings

- The amount of contact foster children have with their parents has increased considerably since the Children Act 1989.

- Home was the most popular meeting place for children and families.

- Carers were more likely to promote contact if they were trained, understood the purpose of contact, had a good relationship with the child and felt well supported.

- Indirect contact was also important to keep emotional links alive.

- Parental contact was positively associated with the child's behaviour and well-being when fostered and with reunification.

THE FREQUENCY OF CONTACT

The implementation of the Children Act 1989 has had a fundamental impact on contact between foster children and their families. Prior to the Act only some 11 per cent of the children saw their parents on a weekly basis. Findings from the survey of social work files suggest that this has increased fourfold. Nonetheless, the proportion of children (a third) who were not in contact with a parent has changed little, although only 17 per cent were cut off entirely from all their family members. Contact with mothers was most common (nearly two thirds of the children) followed by contact with separated siblings (nearly half). Visits with fathers were less common and rarely occurred when families had broken up. Although contact with wider kin was not the norm, a fifth of the children saw a grandparent, aunt or uncle. The greater emphasis since the Children Act on ensuring stability of education for looked-after children also meant that most foster children were able to continue their school-based friendships with peers and teachers.

THE VENUE FOR CONTACT

The survey of social work case files showed that approximately half of the sample either saw their family at home (24%) or at the foster home (23%). Social services venues, such as nurseries or family centres, served as meeting places for the children and their families in 38 per cent of the cases. The qualitative study found that both the children and the parents valued home visits because they offered continuity. Children were able to see other relatives and friends, re-acquaint themselves with their neighbourhood and engage in typical family activities, while parents were enabled to continue actively to parent their child. Contact at the foster home was met with mixed feelings: children were often positive, but parents expressed less satisfaction and often resented carers for usurping their role. Social services venues were generally used when contact required supervision. Supervised contact was often brokered with parents in order to avoid a care order and more formal restrictions. Social services venues were seldom popular meeting places because they offered little privacy and restricted everyday family interactions.

PARTNERSHIP WITH PARENTS

The majority of families in the study were experiencing considerable adversity, and social workers encountered a great deal of difficulty in translating the Children Act principle of working in partnership with parents into practice. The findings from the qualitative study suggest greater levels of involvement by parents in some aspects of the planning process than in others. Few parents felt they had any control over whether or not their child was looked after or whom the child should live with. Moreover, parents were rarely actively involved in preparing their child for the placement or accompanying the child to the foster home. But working in partnership with parents proved important because involvement in early decisions about placement and contact was positively associated with parents remaining in contact with their children.

SUPPORTING CONTACT

Social services departments played an important role in promoting and supporting contact. Regular social work visits to parents were associated with continued parental contact with children. With regard to the contact visits themselves, social services enabled contact through supplying the venues and resourcing transport. In 60 per cent of the cases included in the qualitative study, parents believed social workers had helped them to keep in touch with their absent child. In contrast, many of the factors associated with lack of parental contact were indicative of chronic parenting difficulties, such as a long history of social services concerns about the child, two or more previous care episodes, the child being subject to a care order, poor attachment and parental drug and alcohol misuse. In such cases, a lack of parental contact may well be appropriate.

INVOLVING CHILDREN IN THE DECISION-MAKING PROCESS

To work in partnership with parents may prove difficult, but ascertaining the child's wishes and feelings (a local authority duty under the Children Act 1989) can be particularly problematic when children's experiences have left them with a deep distrust of adults. Effective communication is especially hard when children are young or have communication difficulties. The findings from the qualitative study of children aged 5–12 suggest that in two thirds of the cases children were ill informed about their forthcoming placement, and only half of the children fostered with strangers had met their prospective carers prior to placement.

INDIRECT CONTACT

Contact between the children and their families were not restricted to visiting. Links were also kept alive through thoughts and feelings and through more physical methods such as telephoning and letter writing. Emotional ties were also strengthened through special activities and projects, such as treasured toys, photographs and clothing. In half of the cases telephones were regularly used to connect children and families. Calls were a source of information and reassurance. Postal contact, although not common, was highly prized. The low rate of letter writing should be set within the context of frequent visiting and high levels of parental illiteracy. Talking is a further way in which bonds of affiliation may be kept alive, and around half of the children talked to someone about home and family. The qualities that children valued in deciding to whom to talk included friendliness, trust, empathy and a willingness to listen.

THE ROLE OF FOSTER CARERS

The principle of contact between children and their families was accepted by all foster carers. When parental contact ceased, this was usually the result of the parents' behaviour and wishes rather than because carers blocked or hindered contact. However, contact was rarely a trouble-free process. Three types of problems dominated the carers' perception of contact: parents who demanded too much of carers' time for their own needs; parents who played the child off against the carer; and erratic and unreliable visiting. The role carers played in contact arrangements varied, but a number of factors were associated with carers promoting contact: formal training, a shared understanding with social workers of the aim and duration of placement and purpose of contact, a good relationship with the child and being well supported themselves.

OUTCOMES

The survey of social work files showed that four years after admission 41 per cent of the children were living at home or with relatives, 25 per cent were with their original carers, 5 per cent were living independently, 12 per cent had been adopted and 17 per cent were living with new carers or in residential care. The factors associated with children's well-being and adjustment while fostered were strong parent/child attachment relationships and continued parental contact. These were also associated with the likelihood of reunification.

The qualitative study suggested that a return home might not always be in the child's best interests. In half of the cases the parent/child relationship remained problematic, with parents, carers and social workers holding reservations about the homecoming. Return was more successful when the following factors applied: good parent/child attachment, well-motivated parent(s), well-resourced and purposive contact, the contact was a positive experience for both parent and child and the return was part of a shared plan. In more than half of the cases included in the qualitative sample, children had experienced a change of placement. For many children a single, well-planned placement move, particularly when children went to live with relatives, had a positive impact on their well-being and benefited contact. Although a stable placement has frequently been used as an indicator of a successful placement, the findings from the qualitative study suggest this presumption is unsafe. While half of the children in stable placements improved their relationship with their carers, the remaining children failed to form a secure, stable, affectionate relationship.

Messages for policy and practice

Accommodation is generally used as a service of last resort. To set accommodation within the context of family support would encourage a more imaginative attitude to contact. In cases where parents' chronic difficulties prevent them from fully parenting their child but there is evidence of good attachments, accommodation and contact should be used to promote on-going shared care arrangements.

Fostering Adolescents[3]

Elaine Farmer, Sue Moyers and Jo Lipscombe
School for Policy Studies, University of Bristol

There is little information about what makes some carers particularly successful in looking after young people or which services make a real difference. This study examined how supports for foster carers and their parenting approaches relate to outcomes for adolescents.

Study design

Sixty-eight young people aged 11 to 17 were selected from 14 local authorities and 2 independent fostering agencies. All the placements were intended to be medium to long term and arose at least partly from concerns about the behaviour or emotional well-being of the young person. Data were collected through a review of case files and interviews with the young people, their foster carers and social workers at the beginning of the placement and again 12 months later or at placement ending if this occurred earlier.

The data included background information on past adversities, involvement with social services and care histories. Measures of the young people's behaviour, depression, and peer involvement and of carer stress and functioning were collected at the beginning and at follow-up. The main measures of outcome were 'success' (placement continuing well at outcome or a positive ending) and placement breakdown.

At the end of the year 56 per cent of placements had not disrupted and 47 per cent were rated successful. Young people who did well on these outcomes were compared with those who did not.

Key findings
CARERS AND SUPPORT

Carers experienced support services as a 'net' that was only as strong as its weakest link. Generally, they appreciated family placement workers and carer groups (important to half the carers). However, they were critical of young people's social workers and out-of-hours services (unless provided by the family placement service). Seventy per cent of carers reported difficulties in contacting social workers and in a fifth of cases contact between the social worker and young person was less than monthly. In contrast, carers felt better supported when the young person was receiving appropriate counselling.

Single carers (31% of the sample) were at a particular disadvantage, having weaker social support networks but receiving less training, lower levels of local authority services and less support from local professionals than the foster carer couples. The pressures of work and finding a childminder could make it difficult for them to support the young person's education or attend groups, which were not always seen as geared to their needs. Friends were therefore particularly important to this group.

There was room for concern about the overall level and targeting of support. Frequent social work visits were associated with low levels of carer stress. However, social workers provided most support to those carers who were best supported in other ways. Efforts to improve one element of support (e.g. the out-of-hours service) by cutting back on others (e.g. the family placement service) were not appreciated. Just under half (44%) of the foster carers felt that their views were seldom or never taken seriously within social services and fewer than half (46%) felt that they were an important member of the team which had responsibility for the young person.

RESPONSIBILITY FOR KEY TASKS

There were gaps in the practice of this sample of experienced foster carers. In some cases these may reflect lack of training and in others a lack of clarity over the relative responsibilities of carers and social workers.

- Two fifths of the carers did not discuss sexual health or sexuality with the young people even though many looked-after young people are poorly informed about normal sexual development, sexual health and contraception.

- Half of the foster carers had little involvement with schools, including 20 who reported having no contact with the young people's schoolteachers.

- Two fifths of the carers showed little encouragement for the young people to develop age-appropriate life skills such as budgeting, helping with cooking meals and completing forms, that would prepare them for leaving care and later life.

- Foster carers were significantly less sensitive to the needs and anxieties of girls than boys. The interviews revealed a small number of girls whose worries and real unhappiness about their placements were not apparent to their foster carers.

PLACEMENT PROCESS AND OUTCOMES

The young people did not feel much involved in pre-placement decisions and wanted more information about the foster families before they moved. Placements were more likely to disrupt when carers' preferences for a male or female young person had been overridden and they had received inadequate information on the young person's difficulties and plans for education and long-term care before the placement started.

YOUNG PEOPLE'S CHARACTERISTICS AND OUTCOMES

Young people with histories of aggressive behaviour, with low confidence in schoolwork or with no attachment to an adult before the placement (for example, because of failed adoption or long-term care) experienced increased levels of disruption. Those who were confident about their social relationships at school were more likely to be successful as were those who had particular skills and interests. Hyperactivity and conduct problems in the placement predicted poor outcomes, as did a judgement that the young people had a negative impact on the other children in the placement. Carers were unwilling to tolerate placements that caused serious problems for others in the household even though they were generally tolerant of other kinds of difficulty.

CARERS AND OUTCOMES

Two fifths (41%) of the carers had experienced four or more sizeable stresses (e.g. bereavement or placement breakdown) in the six months prior to the placement. Strained carers responded less sensitively to the young people, disliked them more often and showed them less warmth. Their foster children had worse outcomes, as indeed did those with carers who had experienced stresses before the placement.

In keeping with these findings, outcomes were poorer when carers received little social work support and particularly so when they felt that needed specialist support had not been forthcoming. In contrast, carers who received a lot of support from their own resident or local children had fewer disruptions. Placements were significantly more likely to be successful when the carers reported receiving substantial support from family members, from their social networks or from local professionals, or that they had found social work help to be particularly useful.

In general there were fewer disruptions when at first interview:

- the foster carers had been able to respond to the young people's 'emotional age' when it was considerably younger than their chronological age (e.g. by providing opportunities for play and nurture generally appropriate to a younger child)

- the young people had been able to talk about their past histories with their carers (or indeed to confide in others).

Placements were also more successful when:

- the foster carers had given a moderate level of encouragement to young people to learn life skills that would prepare them for leaving care and later life, such as budgeting, helping with cooking meals and completing forms

- the carers monitored the activities of the young people when they were outside the house.

CONTACT AND OUTCOMES

The widespread idea that adolescents can manage their own contact was not borne out in the study. Almost two thirds of the young people had contact with someone in their network that was detrimental to them. The main problems were repeated rejections, parental unreliability and exposure to abuse. Young people reacted to these problems with distress and difficult behaviour. A minority (13%) of young people had no family contacts but only one of these had an independent visitor. Difficulties with contact were rarely resolved over the course of placements and were significantly related to higher disruption rates.

In a few cases social workers had taken action to improve contact, usually by arranging for contact that was less frequent but of a higher quality or by involving another family member, like a grandparent or aunt, who could provide attention and nurture. Contacts with maternal grandparents were a particularly important source of support.

Messages for policy and practice

- Good support services were linked to reduced foster carer strain and hence to better outcomes for fostered adolescents. There should therefore be better support for carers, including regular contact with social workers, responsive out-of-hours services, attention throughout the placement to the problems of carers' children and the provision of full information about young people before placement.

- There should be particular attention to the needs of single carers, carers under strain before the placement and carers taking hyperactive foster children. Paid breaks, intensive support packages, dedicated respite care and placement of 'easier' young people with strained carers may all have a role.

- Clarification of responsibility and accountability for key tasks such as sex education, educational involvement and life skills are needed.

- Training, recruitment and support for foster carers should include a focus on the key parenting skills identified in the study. This would include dealing with contact, responding to the young person's emotional age, talking to young people about the past and monitoring activities outside the home.

- The impact of school on the placement and vice versa needs particular recognition.

- Counselling and other specialist help for fostered teenagers is associated with the maintenance of placements, and foster carers' requests for such help should always be taken seriously.

- More proactive work is required in relation to contact with family members, in particular in helping young people to cope with continuing parental rejection, ambivalence or unreliability and in encouraging the involvement of relatives who can offer them more positive relationships.

Family and Friends Carers: Scoping paper prepared for the Department of Health[4]

Joan Hunt
Department of Social Policy and Social Work, University of Oxford

This paper was commissioned by the Department of Health to inform the policy-making process in relation to a particular form of substitute care: that provided by members of children's extended families or social network. It includes carers who are approved as foster carers but also covers those who are providing care outside the looked-after system.

Study design

Family and friends care is an under-developed area of policy and practice despite being clearly prioritised in the Children Act 1989 and there have been few UK research studies on the topic. There is, however, a burgeoning international literature. The brief, therefore, was:

- to describe the current policy and legislative framework, highlighting any anomalies, difficulties or conflicts

- to review the existing research evidence, including evidence from the United States and New Zealand, in relation to the policy and practice issues and policy and legislative framework

- to analyse the implications for policy development, particularly in relation to children's services objectives

- to describe the forthcoming research evidence

- to identify the gaps in the research evidence.

The paper is divided into three main sections. The first considers the research evidence relating to kinship care and the well-being of children. The second outlines the policy and legislative framework and the issues identified in the research literature. The third examines what further research is needed. There is an extensive bibliography and summaries of the research design of British studies, published, unpublished and in progress at the point the paper was submitted.

Key findings

The research evidence for the actual and potential benefits of family and friends care is fragmentary, not always as reliable or useful as might be wished and in some respects contradictory. Nonetheless, the weight of the evidence tends towards the positive.

On a range of measures – health, education, emotional and behavioural development – children appear to do about as well as those in stranger foster care, with some studies suggesting they may do better and only a few worse. Children are generally reported to feel secure, happy, integrated and safe.

Many characteristic features of family and friends care (carer commitment, placement stability, continuity of experiences and relationships, family contact) are usually regarded as being more likely to produce good outcomes.

There is little evidence to support concern about the quality of care provided in more than a minority of cases, although parental contact can be difficult and breach of contact restrictions a problem.

There is scope to extend the use of family and friends placements, as an alternative to care and as a care option. Usage across the country appears to be highly variable.

Family and friends care will not be appropriate for all children. Research can currently offer little guidance on predictive factors. Assessment is crucial but forms of assessment used for stranger carers may be inappropriate.

Family and friends carers are inadequately supported. The children have similar needs to those placed with stranger foster carers and carers tend to be more disadvantaged, untrained and unprepared. There is a huge gap between need and provision across the whole spectrum of care arrangements with even those registered as foster carers generally receiving an inferior service. Finance is a major issue.

Family and friends care is a challenging and relatively unfamiliar area of work for social workers. It is different from, and potentially more difficult to work with than, traditional foster care. Practitioners are likely to need training and support to understand the unique features of this form of care and develop the special skills and knowledge it demands.

Messages for policy and practice

There are no grounds for calling into question the Children Act philosophy that where children cannot live with their birth parents the extended family should be the first port of call. There is, however, an urgent need for policy development to reinforce this objective and enable it to be delivered more effectively. A consistent theme in research is that family and friends care is a distinctive form of care which requires its own policy and practice guidance, systems, structures and services tailored to the particular needs of these families. Very little of this is yet in place.

ACTION POINTS FOR CENTRAL GOVERNMENT

- *A focused and coordinated cross-government initiative* is needed to take forward this area of work, something like a task force on kinship care. Compared with the attention that has been given to residential care and, latterly, adoption, kinship care is clearly the 'poor relation'. Such a body could institute a widespread consultation exercise on kinship care, stimulate debate and provide the drive to address the many difficult issues inherent in this form of child care provision.

- *Financial support must be addressed as a matter of urgency.* Levels of support are inadequate and the multiplicity of options confusing and difficult to access. Local authority provision is inconsistent and not transparent.

- *Service provision.* Developing a framework for providing a higher and more consistent level of service provision should also be a priority. Consideration could be given to including kinship care within the carer's legislation so that carers would be entitled at least to an assessment of need. This would also have the advantage of moving the emphasis away from kinship care as a type of fostering to seeing it as primarily a form of community care which should not have to compete for funds with children's placement services.

Within the current system government could take a lead, as has been done with disabled children, in specifying that children living with kinship carers, as a group, should be regarded as potentially in need. Government could also assist by ensuring that services with which kinship carers are most likely to come into contact are geared up to responding appropriately. This would apply to the Benefits Agency, for example, schools and health services, as well as initiatives aimed at 'ordinary' parents, such as Sure Start and Parentline Plus.

- *Information* – central government needs to take the lead in making kinship care more visible by devising mechanisms for collecting data on the whole population of children who are living with relative carers. A relatively simple first step would be to identify this group specifically within the data collected on children in need.

- *Research and training* – government also needs to commission and disseminate research on kinship care to inform policy and practice and work with local authorities and higher education institutions on the incorporation of this area of work into basic, post-professional and in-service training. It could also usefully encourage the sharing of information, practice developments and issues, for instance through a website.

- *Action points for local government* – it is clear that local policies need to be developed on an inter-departmental and inter-agency basis, ensuring that Children's Services Plans take account of the particular needs of children in kinship care. However, the main burden is likely to fall on social services.

- *Valuing the extended family* – effective policies and practice have to grow out of valuing what kinship carers do, appreciating their difficulties and understanding that this form of care is unique. Some of the research suggests that there is a fundamental ambivalence about kinship care running through social services departments. This needs to be openly addressed. Social workers need training in what is a significantly different area of work.

- *Raising the profile of kinship care* – this requires good information, at least about the population of carers already involved with social services. Clear policies need to be developed in relation to the provision of financial support and other services. And they need to be publicised: rationing through ignorance cannot be acceptable.

- *Allocating responsibility* for this area of service development, perhaps through the use of designated workers or dedicated units.

- *Creative thinking and consultation about service delivery* – on the whole carers seem to value social work support and want more, not less. But this may not need to be provided in the same way. Some carers may need and want a link worker. At the other end of the spectrum, some carers may just want a clear point of access in order to tap into support at the point they feel they need information or assistance. Local authorities need to consult a wide range of carers from different ethnic groups about their needs and the most appropriate way of delivering services. The possible role of voluntary and community organisations should be investigated.

Remuneration and Performance in Foster Care: Report to Department for Education and Skills[5]

Derek Kirton, Jennifer Beecham and Kate Ogilvie
School of Social Policy, Sociology and Social Research, University of Kent

The principal aim of the project was to explore the relationship between remuneration and other resources available to foster carers and the performance of fostering services. The project was in two stages, the first of which comprised a national analysis seeking to explore at a 'macro' level the relationship between expenditure and performance. The second entailed a more in-depth investigation in selected fostering agencies.

Study design

Stage 1 of the project was based on all local authorities (LAs) in England. From the analysis, 16 local authorities were chosen for Stage 2 based on varying combinations on the axes of carer remuneration and performance (the latter judged on measures of the number and stability of foster placements). For comparison and to represent this growing sector, five independent fostering agencies (IFAs) were also included.

In Stage 1 the researchers used multivariate analysis to relate data on populations of looked-after children to expenditure and fostering performance indicators.

In Stage 2 investigations employed the following methods:

- semi-structured interviews with service managers
- focus group discussions with family placement workers and foster carers
- questionnaire for foster carers (sample c. 2000)
- data on agency performance indicators.

Key findings

At Stage 1, two main hypotheses were tested:

- In local authorities facing greater demands in terms of the size and make-up of their looked-after populations, fostering services would not perform as well as in those facing lesser demands.
- Higher spending on fostering and other children's services would be associated with better foster care performance.

There was some evidence to support both these hypotheses in respect of local authorities' ability to place children in foster care but the combined influence of demand and expenditure factors explained slightly less than half the variation in placement rates.

The Stage 2 survey of foster carers found that while the foster carer population has become more diverse in terms of age, ethnicity and marital status, it is still not fully representative of the wider community. Around a third of female carers and two thirds of male carers have employment outside their foster care duties. However, 70 per cent of carers reported household income from non-fostering sources as being under £20,000.

Relatively few carers are highly money-oriented, but the value context for foster care is changing, with altruistic motivation tempered by expectations of reasonable financial reward and recompense. Foster care is increasingly seen as 'employment' and 61 per cent of carers support the idea that foster care should be salaried. Within local authorities, only 39 per cent of local authority carers expressed satisfaction with their remuneration. Arrangements for additional payments (e.g.

birthdays, holidays or incidental expenditure) and efficiency in dealing with payments played an important part in carers' satisfaction.

Overall, 55 per cent of carers rated their support as good or very good and there were strong links between feelings of support and satisfaction with payment. Only a minority of carers would favour higher payment if this meant less support. Support was found to be closely linked to 'service delivery' in respect of supervising social worker (SSW) visits, reviews, attendance at support groups, and subjective views about 'being listened to'. Feeling supported by the fostering agency was found to be part of virtuous circles linked to participation in support groups, training, social events and a culture in which carers feel valued and listened to. However, less than half of carers said they felt valued and even fewer, 32 per cent, that their agency listened to and responded to their concerns. An important finding was that carers in IFAs generally expressed greater satisfaction than their LA counterparts in relation to payment, support and feeling valued.

Participation in and satisfaction with training were found to be fairly high but not generally linked to carers' satisfaction with their payments. Neither were levels of participation in training found to be associated with the major measures of performance, at least in an aggregated form.

The study also provided some relevant findings on the relationship between remuneration and the likelihood of foster carers adopting looked-after children. Adopting foster carers tended to be more deeply involved in foster care, as judged by length of fostering career, number and range of placements, lack of alternative employment and participation in fostering activities. They also appeared to show less concern with the financial aspects of foster care. However, a third of those not adopting gave financial reasons as (part of) their explanation. Loss of support was cited almost as often. Carers considering or pursuing adoption were less likely to feel valued by social workers, perhaps suggesting that they had a desire for greater autonomy through adopting.

Messages for policy and practice

This research project focused on the position of foster carers and not directly on outcomes for children and young people. There is reason to believe that improved services for the former will benefit the latter but the relationship between expenditure on foster care and (childcare) outcomes is clearly a complex one. In relation to foster carers, the study found evidence that remuneration and other resources are important for carers' satisfaction and feelings of well-being, and for retention of carers. However, the quality of (supportive) relationships and carers' sense of being valued are also important and are dependent to an important degree on good quality practice and management.

Any deployment of resources must be mindful of the necessary balance between remuneration and support(s). There is also scope for measures that will serve to 'value' carers more effectively; these might include the payment of retainers, and prompt/advance payment to avoid carers being 'out of pocket' with expenditure on foster children. It was noteworthy that IFAs rated much more highly in these areas and there is a broader task to consider the wider applicability of IFA measures within foster care.

Helping Foster Carers to Manage Challenging Behaviour: An Evaluation of a Cognitive-behavioural Training Programme for Foster Carers[6]

Geraldine Macdonald and Ioannis Kakavelakis
School for Policy Studies, University of Bristol

Children who are looked after have consistently fared less well than others on a range of indicators, including health, education and social adjustment. One of the factors that appear to increase children's risk of adverse outcomes is lack of placement stability. Placement breakdowns and frequent changes of carer can undermine children's capacity for developing meaningful attachments, disrupt friendships and contribute to discontinuities in education and health care. These breakdowns are often partly brought about by the children's own behavioural and emotional problems.

Against this background the study aimed to improve placement stability through training carers in a 'cognitive-behavioural' approach. This approach requires carers to understand the way children's behaviour is shaped by their environment. Carers identify particular behaviours and seek to understand what prompts them and how their consequences help to maintain them. They then select strategies that may change or reduce the behaviour and monitor how well these work. There is a range of evidence that this approach can be effective both within foster care and more generally.

Study design

The study employed a 'random controlled design'. Carers who volunteered for the study were randomly allocated to a 'training group' (n = 67) and a control group (n = 50). Those in the control group were told that should the training prove effective they would be trained in their turn.

The training was provided to six different groups of foster carers by an experienced clinical psychologist and a professor of social work. Initially it involved five weekly three-hour sessions followed by a follow-up session. This was later changed to four weekly five-hour sessions followed by a follow-up. The style was 'collaborative' and sought to reflect both the constraints facing foster carers and their expertise. Each participant also had a 'course handbook' and was expected to carry out homework.

The basic question was whether the training programme would enable carers to use it effectively. More specifically, it was expected that carers trained in this way would know more about the approach, use it more often, and reduce both the number of behavioural problems that they encountered and the breakdowns these could produce. They should also report success and greater confidence in dealing with behavioural difficulties.

These hypotheses were tested by comparisons between the training and control groups using data provided by interviews before training and six months after its completion. These interviews provided measures of carer satisfaction, child behaviour, placement breakdown and knowledge of behavioural principles.

Key findings

In comparison with the control group the training group was very satisfied with the programme and almost all would recommend or strongly recommend it to others. They increased their knowledge of behavioural principles and became more confident in dealing with difficult behaviour. In some ways they became more likely to use a behavioural approach but the evidence on this was not consistent. They did not apparently reduce the incidence of behavioural problems, or placement breakdown.

The apparent failure of the programme to achieve its main aims may have reflected a variety of pressures. The programme itself may need modification so that there is more emphasis on the skills of delivering the interventions. It could also with benefit be more intensive – that is, delivered in smaller groups to carers who were enabled to attend more regularly and to complete their homework. Some carers might also benefit from individual rather than group training. In addition, foster children have faced very serious difficulties and may need other interventions over and above 'behavioural management'.

Messages for policy and practice

The evaluation suggests that the programme was not effective in achieving a majority of its aims. There are, however, indications that this might have been attributable, at least in part to:

1.   some organisational difficulties which impacted upon the strength of the study to address those aims

2.   limitations in the length and effective content of the programme, and

3.   a lack of available support within the agencies to help foster carers implement newly acquired skills.

In terms of the perceived need for such training, the carers' overall satisfaction with the programme and the evidence from course tasks suggest that the programme was seen as a significant source of advice, knowledge and skills development. Many carers commented that the programme should be a requirement of all new foster carers.

More generally, the study provides no grounds for thinking that training is not necessary. There is abundant evidence that carers have a very important impact on the quality of placements. Training must be one of the ways of enhancing their contribution. What the study does show is that the fact that training is *prima facie* a good thing does not mean that it necessarily works. More usual methods of evaluation would almost certainly have led to the conclusion that this form of training was a great success. The great merit of the design was to show that while this form of training is sensible it is almost certainly very difficult to implement successfully. In this way it emphasises the crucial importance of developing this and other forms of training and then subjecting them to equally rigorous test.

Joining New Families: A Study of Adoption and Fostering in Middle Childhood[7]

David Quinton
School for Policy Studies, University of Bristol
Alan Rushton, Cherilyn Dance and Deborah Mayes
Institute of Psychiatry, King's College London

Study design

This study was conducted in the early 1990s when it was evident that children adopted from care were forming a growing proportion of the adopted population. It was known that the older these children were when they joined a new family, and the more behavioural difficulties they had, the greater was the risk of poorer outcomes. Earlier research had suggested that although the level of behavioural problems was a risk these could be managed in adoptive families in the context of a strong mutual relationship between family and child.

It was important, therefore, to understand more about what was happening within permanent families when older children were placed. How did family members and the incoming children negotiate the tasks of integration into a new and different family structure? What kinds of behavioural difficulties were most prominent? Which of these tended to be persistent and which were associated with particular difficulties for parents? What forms of help were social workers able to offer and what other supports were needed?

Accordingly, with the collaboration of 18 local authorities in and around London, 84 children between five and nine years old were identified, for whom the plan was permanence with a new and unrelated family, with or without a view to adoption. Sixty-one families agreed to take part in face-to-face interviews at 1, 6 and 12 months following placement. In addition, social workers for both the children (child's social worker) and family (family social worker) were interviewed at the 1- and 12-month points. Some of the 61 index children moved to their new placement with one or more siblings. In these cases just one child in the age range was selected as the focus of the interviews.

Sample characteristics

The sample was fairly evenly split between girls and boys and their mean age at placement was seven years five months (range 59–121 months). Most of the children were white and were placed with white families. Two children had both parents of African-Caribbean origin and eight were of mixed parentage. There were varying degrees of precision in matching the characteristics of the birth parents and grandparents with the ethnic, cultural and religious characteristics of the new parents. Of the ten children with at least one parent of ethnic minority origin, half were placed with families who had similar ethnic backgrounds.

The backgrounds of the children's birth families were characterised by marital difficulties (57%), poor material circumstances (62%), financial hardship (62%), major psychiatric disorder (22% of mothers, 13% of fathers) and alcohol and drug problems (38% of mothers, 53% of fathers). The majority of the children had suffered some form of abuse or neglect and some had experienced multiple abuse. The mean number of previous placements was 6.7 with a range from 1 to 19. The cases of those who had experienced many moves were characterised by frequent attempts to restore children to their birth families.

The mean age of the new mothers and fathers was 39 and 41 respectively. Only three new families were headed by a lone mother and one by a lone father. The majority were couples who had been living together for an average of 14 years (range 3–25). Thirty-nine of the index children were placed singly, although many had siblings who were placed elsewhere. Most of the singly placed (30) joined families who already had children at home. The remaining 22 index children were placed with at least one brother or sister and most of these sibling groups joined families without resident children at the time of placement.

Each of the interviews with new parents covered a range of aspects of family life: the behaviour and friendships of the placed children at home and at school, the development of relationships within the family, the parents' assessments of the progress of the placement, the level and type of contact with social workers and other supportive agencies, and the parents' views on their need for support. The level of emotional and behavioural problems displayed by the children at home were assessed using a standard checklist.

The initial interview with the children's social workers (CSWs) provided a detailed account of the pre-placement experiences of each of the index children. This included not only events leading up to their being looked after, but their time in foster or residential care and the amount of work done with them in preparation for their permanent placement. Family social workers (FSWs) described their assessment and preparation work with the new family and both workers explained their plans for supporting the placement. At the one-year interview both CSWs and FSWs provided an account of the support that they considered had been needed and what had been provided, as well as their views on the progress made.

Key findings

There were only three disruptions during the first year, but it was clear that continuing placements varied substantially in the degree to which the parents viewed the experience as positive for themselves or the children. Overall, the placement was considered successful in the majority of cases, with nearly three quarters of the children forming sound relationships with their new families who reported reasonably high levels of satisfaction.

The parents' free accounts of the behaviours they found challenging or stressful focused on conduct problems or opposition from the children. However, the systematic questioning about behaviour revealed that as a group the children also showed high levels of over-activity. The sample showed little change in their behaviour problems over the first year when considered as a group, although this apparent similarity masked significant changes in both directions for different sub-groups of children. Some showed substantial improvements while the behaviour of other children deteriorated markedly. There was a significant tendency for improvements in behavioural problems to be associated with stable placements, but not exclusively so. A proportion of parents remained committed to and bonded with their child despite increasing behavioural problems. However, the majority of those children whose placements were considered less stable showed deteriorating behaviour patterns.

When outcomes were examined according to different characteristics of the placements and the children, poorer outcomes were found to be more likely for children who were placed singly with established families. A number of factors, which were found to predict less good outcomes, tended to be concentrated in this type of placement. These included the child having been actively rejected by the birth parents, the presence of marked restlessness or distractible behaviour, and parents who found it hard to maintain a warm and sensitive response to the child in the early weeks of placement. The analyses indicated that once these three factors were taken into account, the type of placement ceased to make a difference.

The relationships between the incoming child and other children in the household was one of the major concerns that the parents reported. As might be expected, problems of this nature were more common when children were close in age. However, larger age gaps did not necessarily mean a smooth transition, although there was less likelihood of parents anticipating that these difficulties could lead to a disruption.

Although difficulties at school were not necessarily associated with placement outcomes these were another source of significant concern for a number of parents. Information from teachers showed that the behaviour of many of the children in school was significantly more difficult than that of comparison children, and again poor concentration and restlessness were marked problems. In addition, a number of the children entered their new schools with considerable learning problems that had not previously been recognised. Many of the parents of these children felt that they needed substantial support in securing the educational provision that their child required.

The quality of the contribution of both the child's social worker and the family social worker was categorised and associations with outcome were explored. No statistically significant associations were found for the pre-placement preparatory work, but during the year the most intensive family social worker service was allocated to the most problematic placements.

Overall, the study confirms that, even for highly disturbed children who pose a considerable challenge to new parents, permanent substitute care can result in stable placements for the majority by the end of the first year.

Siblings in Late Permanent Placements[8]

Alan Rushton, Cherilyn Dance and Deborah Mayes
Institute of Psychiatry, King's College London
David Quinton
School for Policy Studies, University of Bristol

Previous studies have examined relative *outcomes* for sibling groups compared with singleton placements but this study, in addition, explores the sibling relationships of children being placed permanently from care. A fifth (21%) of these placements involved foster care and the remainder adoption.

The aims of the study were to:

- investigate the location, circumstances and contact arrangements of birth siblings who were not with the placed children

- study factors influencing social work decisions about the separation, reunion or maintenance of the sibling group

- examine placement outcomes for individual children of a similar age according to whether they were placed with or without siblings

- explore the character of relationships between children in different types of placement

- examine the sibling relationships of children placed together from care in comparison with those of children growing up in their own families

- investigate the impact of placement on the birth children of the new families

- document the level of social work intervention with particular reference to sibling factors.

These data were drawn from a prospective, longitudinal study of children placed for permanence with new, unrelated families. At least one child placed with each new family was between 5 and 11 years of age at the time of placement. Placements that included a child with a profound mental or physical disability were excluded from the sample. Referrals were received over a 21-month period in 1994–5 from local authorities and voluntary agencies in England who agreed to participate in the study.

Seventy-two families took part in the study. They had 133 children placed with them. The new parents were interviewed about all of the children in their family (including their birth children) at 3 and 12 months after placement. The family social worker (FSW) and the children's social worker (CSW) for each case were also interviewed at both the beginning and the end of the year.

The interview with the parent included a section on the interaction between siblings, and they also completed a sibling-relationship questionnaire. The CSW interview included questions on decision-making in regard to separating or maintaining sibling groups both in the past and present; on the whereabouts of siblings elsewhere and the arrangements for contact between the children. In addition, a group of 100 birth parents recruited from two schools completed the same questionnaire as the sample parents to enable comparisons to be made on behaviour and sibling interactions.

The sample was composed of three groups:

- 19 children placed singly in child-free families

- children placed singly with established families

- 40 sibling groups placed with new families.

Although the singly placed children were all between 5 and 11 years of age, the sibling groups included children outside this age range in both directions.

The children's sibling networks, decision-making and contact arrangements

There were 32 singly placed children and 40 sibling groups (varying in size between two and four). Most of the children in sibling group placements were full siblings. In 48 of the 72 placements, children had other siblings, of dependent age, who were elsewhere (see Table A1). Siblings who remained with their birth parents were significantly more likely to be much younger children and they were very often half-siblings to the placed children. All but one of the 11 singletons who had other siblings in care had lived with them at some point in their care histories but, on average, had been on their own for two years. Sibling groups tended to have been together for most of their time in care.

Table A1 Placed children and siblings elsewhere					
Placement type	No other siblings	Siblings with birth family	Siblings in care elsewhere	Siblings with birth family and in care	Total
Singly placed child	8	13	6	5	32
Sibling group	16	11	9	4	40

The decisions made about the permanent placement maintained previous constellations in 80 per cent of the cases. Singleton, rather than sibling group, placements had received greater consideration in previous placement choices and in the extent to which a comprehensive sibling assessment had been undertaken. The factors most often mentioned as influential in the decision-making process were the relationship between the siblings, the individual needs of the children, their shared history and the reports from their carers. A full sibling assessment was carried out in only 16 of 48 cases where there was more than one child in care. Sibling assessments had not been carried out in any of the cases described as unstable at the end of the year.

Just over half (58%) of the new parents of children who had siblings placed elsewhere reported some face-to-face contact with them during the first year of placement. In two thirds of cases the contact was described as having had a positive effect on the child/ren. On the whole, sibling contact was not hard for families to manage; only 8 of 26 reported any significant difficulties.

Placement outcome and placement type

Of the 32 singleton placements, 26 (81%) were reported to be stable at the end of the first year, 2 were in difficulty and 4 had disrupted. Thirty-six of the 40 sibling group placements (90%) were satisfactory, two were intact but unstable and two had disrupted. Thus, the sibling placements had a slightly better outcome than the singletons, but not significantly so.

Based on the stability of the placements at the end of the first year, social workers appeared to be making the right decisions about placement patterns for the children in their care. Where changes in the constellation did occur it was more likely to be a reunion than a separation. Where children were reunited (six cases) or separated (two cases) the placements were reportedly stable at the end of the first year. Of the 16 cases where separation was considered and dismissed two were in difficulty at the end of the year and two had disrupted. Of the seven cases where reunion had been resisted, six of the placements were going well.

Sibling interactions

Both in interview and in their responses to the questionnaire, the parents reported high levels of conflict and rivalry among placed sibling groups, and many felt that the children showed little warmth towards each other. Over the course of the year warmth improved and conflict decreased a little, but it remained substantially higher than in the control group. In some cases these disputes between the children could be incessant and extremely worrying, including a minority of siblings who would regularly inflict injury and some who would need to be physically separated from fights. The severity of disputes was significantly associated with the level of strain reported by the parents at the end of the year.

For new sibling relationships, that is those groups involving a placed child joining existing birth children, warmth between the new child and the others tended to be lower throughout than that shown by children in the control group, although it increased over the year. Levels of conflict or dispute were also low in comparison with the control group but rivalry was high, persistent and on a par with that shown amongst placed sibling groups. Whereas rivalry among placed siblings tended to manifest itself in an overt and physical manner, jealousies tended to be expressed in less dramatic ways within new sibling groups.

The impact on birth children

At both interview points, 3 and 12 months after placement, parents were asked what impact the placement had had on their own children and how they had adapted to their new siblings. At the first interview, new parents described the placement as having had little negative effect for 10 of the 28 birth children, minor adjustment problems were described in a further 12 cases and more significant problems in 6 cases. This amounted to 64 per cent who were experiencing some kind of adjustment difficulty. At one year (with losses to the sample) the new parents described adjustment difficulties for 67 per cent. In nine cases these were considered to be relatively minor hiccups, which were discussed in the context of the placement having had a primarily positive impact, but there were more significant difficulties for seven young people.

Social work intervention and siblings

The social workers were clearly faced with difficult decisions in making the placement plan and in deciding what action to take if the plans were not working out well. This suggests that social workers need to think beyond received imperatives about placement policy and consider what specific features justify the placement plan. They need to bear in mind the *quality* of the sibling relationships and have at their disposal the concepts to describe and assess the nature of interactions and to think through *the relationship consequence* of decisions. The capacity to be alert to and to recognise relationship problems is essential if social workers are to have a better grasp of the range of challenges confronting the new parents.

Costs and Outcomes of Non-infant Adoptions: Report to the Department for Education and Skills[9]

Julie Selwyn, Wendy Sturgess, David Quinton and Catherine Baxter
School for Policy Studies, University of Bristol

This study had three main aims:

- to examine why some children were more easily adopted than others

- to estimate the unit costs for adoption

- to consider the support needs of those adopting older, more challenging children.

The study took the opportunity to follow up a complete epidemiological-based sample of 130 older children for whom an adoption best interest decision had been made in the 1990s. A catch-up prospective design was used to track the care careers of the children then aged 3–11 years. Case files were read and current carers (80% of adoptive parents and 74% of foster carers) were interviewed. Ninety-six of the children had been matched with an adoptive family and, of these, 80 were still with their adoptive families at follow-up. This was on average seven years after placement with the children then aged 7–21 years. Of the remaining children, 34 were in long-term foster care or other permanent placement and 16 children had had numerous disruptions, with no stability of care. These three groups (adopted, permanently placed and unstable care career) formed the basis of later analyses of outcomes. This gives the study particular strengths and enables the 'success' of adoption to be more accurately portrayed, as the pathways of all the children could be charted, than when, as is more usual, the outcomes of children already in adoptive families are examined.

Costing data were collected from files, social services departments (SSDs) and during interviews and used to calculate three separate adoption unit costs. First, the cost of placing a child for adoption; second, the cost to social services of supporting a looked-after child in an adoptive placement prior to the adoption order and, last, the cost to social services of providing post-adoption support after the adoption order.

Key findings

- Children came from families with many problems. Alcoholism, substance abuse, mental health problems and learning difficulties were all prevalent. Children's parents (63%) had often spent time in care themselves and 32 per cent had already had a previous child removed. Consequently, 63 per cent of the children were referred to a SSD before or at the time of their birth. Many agencies were involved with these families and resources were used to try to bring about improvement. These were often poorly targeted and continued for years without any evaluation of success being made.

- The majority of the children (90%) had experienced abuse and neglect, with 68 per cent experiencing multiple and severe forms of abuse. Boys were far more likely than girls to experience parental rejection.

- Once the children (aged 1–10 years) became looked after, challenging behaviour and special needs became more evident and, by the time of the best interest decision, 95 per cent of children had at least one special need, with more than half having four or more special needs.

- Delays were evident at every stage. Forty-one per cent of children waited more than two years (ranging from one month to eight years) for a permanency plan to be in place and 11 per cent waited more than two years for their papers to go before the adoption panel.

- The reasons why some children were not adopted are complex. Adopted children were younger at entry to care and subject to speedier decision-making. Delayed entry to care was a significant predictor of placement outcome. The odds of not being adopted increased by 1.8 for every extra year of delay. Children who had unstable care careers were more likely to have mothers who had mental health problems, to have remained at home longer and to have suffered more severe and multiple forms of abuse. Children in long-term foster care were more likely to have learning difficulties and chronic health problems. There were no statistically significant differences in the emotional and behavioural difficulties in the adopted and permanently placed groups.

- The unit cost of finding a new family, placing and supporting a child until an adoption order was £18,167. Children in this sample lived with their adopters on average for two years before the order so the cost of adoption for these older children was £25,827.

- Eighty children were placed with 66 adoptive families, with just over a quarter adopted by their foster carers. There was not one type of family that was more successful than another, but the role of fathers in supporting adoption was under-estimated by agencies.

- At the best interest decision 52 per cent of children were in contact with their birth parents. There was a lack of planning around contact with frequency, quality and impact poorly assessed. At follow-up, contact had changed as teenagers took over their own arrangements through the use of mobile phones. Young people both reduced and increased contact, which was not always approved of by their adopters or social workers.

- Many adopters described feeling abandoned by agencies once the adoption order had been made. At follow-up, 52 per cent had no form of support and 13 per cent received just an allowance. Foster adopters were more likely to be struggling financially and a quarter of all adopters were described as being in debt as a consequence of trying to meet the child's needs.

- At follow-up, a third of adopters reported few problems, a third described family life as a mixture of conflicts and rewards and for the remaining third there were many problems with few or no rewards and with behaviour difficulties escalating. Adopted children's lives were more stable with fewer disruptions than were found among children in other kinds of placements.

- As the adopted children had grown older, more difficulties had emerged. Forty-four per cent of the children had problems in three or more areas. The strongest predictors of difficulties within the adoptive family were the extent of children's conduct problems and over-activity at the time of the best interest decision. There was some evidence that adoption reduced the severity of problems in those without severe overlapping early adversities to a greater extent than was found among children in other types of placement.

- The views of long-term foster carers were very similar to those of adopters with two exceptions. First, they complained bitterly that although they had cared for the child for years they had been given little parental responsibility and, second, that the care system de-stabilised placements by encouraging early planning of independence.

- Sixteen children had found no stable placement. Most were in specialist residential/secure accommodation. Poor assessment and inadequate attention to their educational needs had contributed to their sad outcomes. These children cost seven times more than those who had been adopted and their costs were expected to continue and increase.

Messages for policy and practice

Practice decisions and legal uncertainties clearly have a profound influence on a child's age at entry to care and on delay in addressing their needs both before and after entering the care system. Our research underlines the importance of current policy efforts to achieve early and rigorous risk assessment and swifter decision-making for children.

The introduction of the Assessment Framework should improve the quality of social work assessments but attention also needs to be given to helping social workers analyse the mass of complex and sometimes contradictory information collected. In case files in this study, there was plenty of information but it was rare to see information converted into a clear plan. Interventions were unfocused and continued without being able to evaluate their success. This contributed to delayed decision-making.

There is an urgent need to review the mental health services and therapeutic services for looked-after children. Only 7 per cent of this sample received on-going support from child and adolescent mental health services (CAMHS) while they were looked after although the need was far greater. Many children were exhibiting distressed and distressing behaviour at school and in their foster placements.

The relationships and roles of men in birth and foster/adoptive families were often ignored. In birth families this led to inaccurate assessments and in foster and adoptive families to assumptions about who would be the main carer and to the kinds of support needed. Social workers need to engage with fathers and recognise the important role they play.

Long-term foster carers want to have more parental responsibility for the children in their care and for some Special Guardianship will meet their needs. Authorities also should consider how they can better support young people in placements that continue without a legal order, to provide stability through childhood and beyond.

Foster Carers: Why They Stay and Why They Leave[10]

Ian Sinclair, Ian Gibbs and Kate Wilson
Social Work Research and Development Unit, University of York

There is widespread agreement that there are not enough foster carers. Appropriate support for carers may attract others and help ensure that those currently fostering are less likely to leave. Against this background the study (York study 1) was begun in 1997 in seven local authorities. It aimed to discover:

- what foster carers liked or disliked about fostering
- what support they wanted
- why they stopped fostering or continued to foster
- whether support influenced their likelihood of ceasing to foster.

Study design

The study involved a census of carers (n = 1528) who were then sent a postal questionnaire (944 questionnaires were returned). The carers were followed up after 19 months and comparisons made between those ceasing to foster and the remainder.

Characteristics of carers

The basic characteristics of foster carers were surprisingly similar to those identified in the 1950s and 1980s. In general the structure of their families was more 'traditional' than is common in the general population: a fact which suggests that fostering is not seen as easily fitting in with certain family forms (e.g. two parents with outside work).

Relative carers

Relative carers seemed to be more socially disadvantaged than other carers. They received on average less remuneration and much less training. (Attitudes to the latter varied with some wanting more training and support and others not.) Relative carers were often involved in family quarrels related to fostering, which they found difficult.

Satisfaction and reasons for leaving

The carers themselves generally found fostering very satisfying and were highly committed to their foster children. The proportion 'in post' in one year who were not 'actively fostering' at the same time next year was only around 10 per cent. A key reason why they continued to foster lay in their commitment to their foster children. Many of those planning to leave delayed doing so until the child they were currently fostering moved on.

Those who ceased caring did so for three main reasons:

- a lack of fit between fostering and their family life
- a lack of good support
- difficulties over particular placements.

Some left because *they did not see fostering as fitting in with their lives or need to work.* Some carers said that they were caring while it fitted in with the stage in their family life. Later they might need to take outside work. In keeping with this, inactive foster carers were much more likely to be working than active ones. Carers over the age of 55 were significantly more likely to cease fostering, defining themselves as 'retiring' although still, in some cases, willing to provide other services to foster care.

Other carers left because *they were not well supported.* Carers wanted respect, efficiency, reliable, warm support from social workers, good information on foster children, responsive out-of-hours services, relief breaks when they needed them, information on entitlements, fair remuneration, and an absence of avoidable hassles (e.g. disputes over insurance when their house was damaged).

Carers who were less frequently visited by 'link workers', or had a combination of lower-than-average income from fostering, support from other foster carers and training, were more likely to cease fostering. Support also needed to be adapted to the carer's family situation. For example, the presence or absence of 'informal support' from outside the family was more important in explaining whether lone carers continued to foster than it was for couple carers.

Other carers left because of *developments in a particular placement.* Events such as allegations, contacts with very difficult birth parents or disruption to the family attributed to the foster child could have a devastating effect on carers and their families and were associated with poor mental health. Breakdowns greatly enhanced the likelihood that a carer would leave since they often simultaneously increased motivation to leave and removed the felt obligation to look after a particular foster child.

Messages for policy and practice

The report suggested that support for foster carers needed to be tailored to their particular family situation. It should be based on a combination of regular social work support, a 'professional' package of relevant training, opportunities for contact with other carers in training or groups, and adequate remuneration. It should pay attention to the particular issues raised by carers such as the need for a good after-hours service. Above all, it should be responsive to events.

Foster Placements: Why They Succeed and Why They Fail[11]

Ian Sinclair, Kate Wilson and Ian Gibbs
Social Work Research and Development Unit, University of York

Why do some foster placements succeed and others fail? This is a crucial question for foster care and this study (York study 2) set out to examine it.

Study design

The study focused on a cross-sectional sample of 596 foster children of all ages placed with the foster families studied in the first York study. Comparisons with other studies and national statistics suggested that the sample was representative with the exception that children placed with relatives were under-represented. The aims of the study were to describe the sample, identify factors which led to breakdown and see if additional support might have prevented this.

The main sources of data were a postal survey in 1998 to foster carers, social workers and family placement social workers, and a follow-up survey 14 months later to the same sources. In addition the researchers had 150 questionnaires from foster children describing their experience and carried out 24 case studies (12 'successes' and 12 'less successful').

The two main measures of success were based on the pooled judgements of carers, social workers and supervising social workers. One measure related to whether or not the placement disrupted. The other related to how far the placement was seen as having gone well.

The researchers analysed case studies, and the accounts of children, carers and social workers, to develop hypotheses about what makes for success in foster care. They then used a variety of statistical techniques to test these hypotheses.

Key findings

Five main groups of factors seemed to lead to both forms of success. These related to the characteristics of the child, the characteristics of the foster family, the 'chemistry' between carers and child, how the child fared at school, and contact with the birth family.

CHARACTERISTICS OF CHILD

Children were more likely to experience successful placements and less likely to experience disruptions if they:

- wanted to be in the placement
- had attractive characteristics
- did not score highly on standard measures of disturbance or difficult behaviour.

CHARACTERISTICS OF SUCCESSFUL CARERS

Case studies suggested that a key factor in success was a carer's ability to handle disturbed attachment behaviour and to control the child without making her or him feel rejected. The statistical findings were in keeping with this. Foster carers were more likely to experience successful placements and avoid disruptions if they:

- were rated highly by the social workers for parenting qualities
- were 'child oriented', as judged from responses to a questionnaire
- had experienced relatively few allegations or disruptions in their previous fostering career.

These factors remained important when account was taken of the characteristics of the children.

CHEMISTRY BETWEEN CARERS AND CHILDREN

Some children 'clicked' or 'fitted' with their foster families. In other cases there were spirals of 'rejection'. 'Disturbed' foster children were more likely to be rejected and therefore more likely to experience placement breakdown. Disturbance that had not led to rejection was not associated with breakdown.

SCHOOL

The child's experience at school almost certainly had an effect on how he or she got on in the placement.

- Children who were happy at school and whose carers said they had been able to encourage them over school were more likely to be successful.
- Contact with an educational psychologist was strongly associated with an absence of breakdown and remained so when other factors were taken into account.
- There was some evidence that the apparent impact of the educational psychologist was greater when the carer was committed to the importance of schooling.

CONTACT WITH THE BIRTH FAMILY

Contacts with families were very significant for both the children and their carers.

- Contact with birth families was commonly distressing to children although they generally wanted more of it. They were, however, discriminating over which family members they wished to see and the circumstances in which they wished to see them.
- Where there was strong evidence of prior abuse and no family member was forbidden contact, breakdown was three times more likely than it was where at least one person was forbidden contact. This finding remained when account was taken of background factors such as age and 'disturbance'.

RULES OF THUMB

In general the study did not support traditional 'rules of thumb'. So it did not suggest that 'on average' placements with siblings or in families where there were other birth children, or frequent moves, were necessarily associated with poor outcomes, nor that placements with relatives were associated with better ones. It was, however, clear that in individual cases these aspects of a placement could be very important (e.g. some children pined for siblings).

IMPACT OF PROFESSIONAL HELP

There was also a disappointing lack of evidence for the effectiveness of contacts with professionals. Contact with all forms of therapist, psychologist or psychiatrist except the educational psychologist was associated with poor outcomes. In part this may have been because many contacts were for assessment only and they were most likely to be provided when the placement was in difficulty. Presumably the child had to be in trouble to see these specialists. There was, however, some evidence that behavioural approaches reduced particular behavioural problems.

Messages for policy and practice

The study suggested that it will always be difficult to find close matches for emergency placements. Carers need to be recruited who are prepared to take quite a wide range of children for such placements and keep them for varying lengths of time. Longer-term placements can then be more closely matched.

More generally, the key to successful foster care lay in the child's school experience, relations with the birth family and the quality of foster carers.

- Foster carers need skills in handling attachment, dealing with difficult behaviour, and encouraging and supporting the child at school.

- Social workers need skills in managing contact with birth families, in discussing with children what they really want and in intervening when foster carer and child start to get the worst out of each other.

- School-based packages of support are important and need to be geared to more than the child's academic needs.

The provision of these requirements will depend on the ability to recruit and support good foster carers, on the development of appropriate training for carers and social workers, and on the development of good links between school and carers. The report recommended that work was needed to develop successful methods of recruitment, training and intervention and to try them out on an experimental basis.

Foster Children: Where They Go and How They Get On[12]

Ian Sinclair, Claire Baker, Kate Wilson and Ian Gibbs
Social Work Research and Development Unit, University of York

A successful foster placement does not guarantee a successful life. This study (York study 3) was designed to identify the links between what happens within foster care and what happens after it.

Study design

The 596 foster children studied in the second York study were followed up over three years. The aim was to find out where they went, how they were now doing and what explained these outcomes. The children were a cross-section of those fostered at a particular point in time and traced through local authority records supplemented by telephone enquiries to social workers, after-care workers and others. Questionnaires were sent to the current or latest social workers of all the children, to their current or latest foster carer, to the current carers of all those not in independent living, to foster children and to the young people in independent living. There were also 30 case studies.

Where were the children at follow-up?

A quarter of the sample were still with their 1998 foster carers. The remainder were almost equally divided between new foster carers (15%), adoptive families (15%), their own families (17%) and independent living (18%). A handful were in some form of residential care (4%) or could not be traced (6%).

The likelihood of these different destinations varied with age. Three quarters of those aged less than two in 1998 were adopted, as were 39 per cent of those aged two to five. More than nine out of ten of those adopted came from these age groups. Children of this age were less likely to be adopted if placed with relatives, in close contact with birth family or disabled.

At the other end of the age range those over 14 were overwhelmingly likely to move to independent living. Continuing foster care was mainly reserved for those between 4 and 14.

The chance of returning home did not differ so much by age. Here the reasons seemed to differ, depending on whether the child returned home soon after they entered the sample or later. Early returns usually reflected social work plans. Many later ones occurred through a combination of disruption and the wish of parent and child to be together. Distance between placement and home had a strong impact on frequency of contact but no apparent effect on the likelihood of return.

How did the children get on in the different settings?

At follow-up the researchers asked the social workers to rate the quality of the children's placements. It was striking that they rated all placements from foster care other than adoption as, on average, much less satisfactory than foster care itself. On balance the evidence favoured the more permanent placements. Children on residence orders were more settled than those fostered and were more often expected to stay on after the age of 18. After allowing for age, it seemed that children who were adopted appeared to do slightly better on certain criteria than children who were fostered.

Children returning home or living independently had the greatest difficulties. Compared with apparently similar peers, those returning home were significantly more likely to be re-abused, to show difficult social behaviour and to show little if any improvement in educational performance. Some young people in independent living 'did well'. Typically they were young mothers with babies who got support from their boyfriend and his family or the small group who went to university. Most care leavers, however, experienced a wide variety of troubles including loneliness; debt; insecure, unskilled and poorly paid jobs; depression; and quarrels with their families.

What predicted outcomes within the different settings?

The outcomes for children seemed to depend on their personal characteristics and their current environment.

Important individual characteristics related to what children wanted, their degree of 'disturbance' and their adjustment at school.

- Children who wanted to be in their foster placement in 1998 were more likely to do well there.
- Returns home were probably more likely to succeed if both parent and child had wanted them.
- The child's individual difficulties in 1998, particularly a measure of disturbed ways of relating, predicted difficulties in most settings in 2001 (e.g. foster care, adoption, independent living).
- Various measures of adjustment at school (e.g. whether child was said to be happy there in 1998 or doing well there in 2001) tended to predict outcomes.

Current relationships were also very important. The quality of current caring was related to well-being in settings where there was a current carer. A strong tie with at least one adult was important for those in independent living.

The findings on contact were complex. Unrestricted contact with the birth family in cases where there was strong evidence of prior abuse predicted re-abuse and placement breakdown. Contact with the birth family on its own was associated with re-abuse, partly because some abuse took place on contact, but also because contact was associated with return home which in turn was associated with re-abuse. Re-abuse was associated with increased disturbance.

Permanence in adoption and foster care

The researchers examined how far adoption and foster care offered the child a family that felt and was permanent.

Adoption seemed the most 'permanent' setting. Adopted children were young. None of their placements disrupted. As far as the researchers could tell these placements also tended to achieve psychological permanence in the sense that the children felt they belonged, were treated as members of the family and were not subject to conflicting pressures from birth family. There was less information on the psychological permanence of those returning home. Older children returning home were less likely than younger ones to remain there.

Most children seemed to be settled in fostering. However, some saw it as 'abnormal' and some continued ambivalent relationships with families who would neither let them be in foster care nor have them home. The children varied over how they saw the relationship between fostering and their own family. A minority wanted to leave foster care and have no more to do with their foster family. Some wanted to return home but retain close contact with the foster family. Some wanted to stay with the foster family but remain in close contact with home. Some wanted to get on with their lives in foster care with little contact with their own family.

The likelihood of staying with the same foster carer (as opposed to changing foster carers) was related to factors predicting disruption in the second York study. Children under 11 were quite likely to remain with their carers, but those over this age had a much greater chance of disruption in their placement. In general the *psychological acceptance of foster care* was at odds with its frequent transience. In both the 'career' and placement studies a large minority (over 40%) answering the questionnaires wanted to stay with their foster carers beyond the age of 18. Despite this, only 10 per cent of those aged over 18 in 2001 were with their former foster carers.

Were outcomes influenced by additional support?

Social workers were viewed warily by both birth and adoptive families. This, combined with shortage of resources and the lack of proven methods of intervention, made it difficult for social workers to influence outcomes.

Foster carers seemed a more promising source of potential support for those foster children for whom they had been important. Some continuing contact with foster carers was associated with one measure of success among those adopted. Case studies suggested that in a minority of cases foster carers could provide crucial support for those going home or into independent living.

Messages for policy and practice

The study concluded that foster care for longer-staying children faces a dilemma. In most cases it does not offer a secure family for life. On the other hand, most of those leaving it go home or into independent living. In neither of these settings do they – in the short term at least – do particularly well. Drastic changes to this situation are difficult to bring about. Most foster children do not want to be adopted. It is hard to bring about changes in the children's own families so that they can be safely and satisfactorily brought up there.

Contributions to resolving this dilemma may involve:

- slight increases in the number of children adopted achieved through the accurate and decisive assessment of the chances of rehabilitating young children and through a more widespread willingness to accept and then support carer adoptions

- experiments in providing more consistent and intensive support for the families of children who do return

- changes in foster care itself, enabling it to be 'more normal', enhance the degree to which children stay on within it after they reach the age of 18, and develop the role of foster carers in supporting children after they have left

- the use of US approaches to 'treatment foster care' that includes birth families both to shorten the length of time children spend in foster care and to increase the capacity of their families to cope

- the application of lessons learnt in supporting care leavers at university or those who are young mothers to the support of care leavers in the job market. The latter have lives which are at least as transitional and difficult as other care leavers, and probably more so.

In all settings it is reasonable to pay close attention to the factors that are closely associated with outcomes: what the children want, their situation at school, their relationships with their current carers and their relationships and contact with their own families. These requirements should inform new efforts to support children and be evaluated through research.

Listening to Children's Views of Care and Accommodation, Report to the Department of Health[13]

Tricia Skuse and Harriet Ward
Centre for Child and Family Research, University of Loughborough

Children are, in a sense, the experts on the care system. In the past too little attention has been paid to their views. The present study was designed in part to rectify this situation. It formed part of a larger set of studies designed to help local authorities explore how data gathered in the course of social work interactions with individual children can be aggregated and used at a more strategic level.

The sample was drawn from a cohort of children from six local authorities, who entered care or accommodation between 1 April 1996 and 31 March 1997, and were still in care or accommodation 12 to 24 months later. Children from this group who left the care of six local authorities between 1 April 1998 and September 2000 were invited to participate in follow-up interviews. During this period, 125 of the children and young people in the cohort left care or accommodation. Efforts were made to interview all these young people, but due to difficulties in tracing and accessing them (for details see the original study), a total of 49 were interviewed between 15 and 39 months after leaving care. Twenty-five of these children and young people were interviewed for a second time approximately one year later.

Key findings

- The interviews showed substantial differences between the experiences of small children and teenagers both during and after care or accommodation.

- Interviews with these children and young people clearly showed how their lives, needs and experiences varied immensely. Only by talking to children themselves can we get a sense of these requirements and how their experiences impact on their futures and identities.

- This study provides an invaluable insight into the experiences of the children and young people's lives *before* and *after* leaving care, as well as while they were looked after. Viewed against the wider context of their whole lives, the generally poor outcomes for children and young people in care or accommodation become more understandable, and less pronounced.

- The majority of the children and young people interviewed had valued their time in care or accommodation, believing their lives would have been worse if they had remained with their birth families.

- Young people who thought it was a 'good' thing that they had been looked after thought that the experience had addressed the factors that had precipitated their admission and/or had improved their long-term life chances.

- The three most popular aspects of being looked after were improved material circumstances, individual members of staff and social workers, and the family environment offered by some foster carers.

- The three most unpopular features were homesickness and missing family and friends, the rules and structure of some residential units and foster homes, and the attitudes of staff in some residential units, which were perceived as disparaging.

Messages for policy and practice

The study provides further support for one of the key objectives of Choice Protects – namely, to develop the involvement of children and young people in planning and developing the services that are being provided for them.

Qualitative information from children and young people in this study embellished and sometimes altered the interpretation of quantitative data. The experience of instability was highlighted by their descriptions of how their sense of identity was affected by loss of possessions, friends and contacts as they moved from one placement to another. This demonstrates the importance of using qualitative as well as quantitative information to reshape services, and also shows how listening to service users is an important element in improving the effectiveness of interventions.

Children's comments and views about the quality of different placements, what makes a good social worker and the reasons why they fail or succeed at school are an invaluable source of information that local authorities need to consider in trying to interpret and improve their performance. However, the diversity of children's circumstances, experiences and views means that services need to be tailored to meet the needs of individual children and should not be based on the assumption that one size fits all.

Practitioners and carers need to be aware of the sense of powerlessness felt by many of these young people: consultation about major decisions that could affect their future was often absent. An improved dialogue between services users and practitioners might do much to improve outcomes.

Permanent Family Placement for Children of Minority Ethnic Origin[14]

June Thoburn, Liz Norford and Stephen Parvez Rashid
Centre for Research on the Child and Family, University of East Anglia, Norwich

The aims of the project were to learn more about children of minority ethnic origin placed from care with permanent substitute families not previously known to them. Most were placed for adoption, but a quarter were placed with the intention that they would grow up as members of foster families.

The majority of the children (274) were part of a larger cohort of 1165 'hard to place' children placed from care with permanent substitute families by 24 voluntary agencies between 1980 and 1984. Additional children placed at the same time were recruited to the sample to increase the number of placements with ethnic minority families. Those placed as 'permanent' foster children were on average older (mean age ten) than those placed for adoption (mean age six), the range being between 1 and 17. Twelve (14%) were aged between one and four at placement; 16 (19%) were aged five to nine; and 57 (67%) were aged nine or over. Thus, in terms of age, they were not unlike those needing stable long-term foster placements today. Foster children were more likely than those placed for adoption to be placed with a sibling, to have continuing contact with a birth parent, and to be placed with an ethnically 'matched' family.

Study design

Data were obtained from records and *logit* analysis was used to study any associations between variables and outcome (measured in terms of whether the young person was still a 'family member' between 7 and 15 years after placement). The interview sample comprised 51 young people in respect of whom at least one parent/carer was interviewed, as were 28 of the young people. Others who declined or were too disabled to be interviewed were observed in their families. The interview sample included 22 children who had been placed as foster children (25%). Sixteen of these were in broadly 'matched' placements. For these 51, interviews were analysed thematically and there was a 'researcher rating' of success based on a range of outcome indicators including data from standardised schedules on self-esteem and mental health. Particular emphasis was given to issues of ethnic identity and adoptive/foster identity, and satisfaction with the adoptive/foster family experience.

Key findings

Five of those placed as permanent foster children left care through adoption or residence orders. Almost one in five placed with the intention of adoption were still fostered (by the same parents) when the records were scrutinised. Twenty-four per cent of placements had disrupted (31% of the foster care placements). Interestingly, the highest disruption rate amongst the foster care group was for the, albeit small, number placed between the ages of five and eight (half of these 16 disrupted) compared with 2 of the 12 placed when aged under five (nearly 17%) and 28 per cent of those placed when nine or over. Of those placed for adoption in the five to eight age group, a smaller proportion (23%) had disrupted, but for the 56 placed for adoption in the oldest group, 43 per cent had disrupted. However, when age at placement and other key variables were held constant, there was no difference in disruption rates between foster children and those placed for adoption. Over half of those placed as foster children (45) were over the age of 18 when the outcomes were evaluated and 70 per cent of these were either still living with the foster parents (13) or had set up home on their own or with a partner but were in close touch and able to call on them for support (18).

Four factors were significantly associated with disruption:

- a history of deprivation or abuse prior to placement
- being older at the time of placement (but this difference peaked at age 10 to 11 at placement)
- behavioural or emotional difficulties at the time of placement
- being described at the time of placement as 'institutionalised'.

No association was found between continuing contact and more or less successful outcomes. There was no statistically significant association between family variables and disruption, including whether or not the placement was ethnically 'matched' or 'trans-racial'. However, when gender was introduced into the model, there was a higher success rate for black boys placed with white families than with black families, but the opposite was the case for black girls. (This may be a sample-specific finding but merits further study.) From the qualitative data, the researchers concluded that black and Asian families had an advantage over white families in preparing their children to cope with racist attitudes and behaviour and to grow up with a strong sense of pride in their appearance and heritage. However, with appropriate selection and support, some white families can successfully parent ethnic minority children, especially those living in ethnically diverse communities. Qualitative data pointed to the importance of the child being willing to be placed (although in some cases this was conditional on his or her continuing to see birth family members and not being adopted). For the foster parents 'enjoying a challenge' was frequently mentioned by successful parents, and successful ethnic minority families were strongly motivated to help a child of their own ethnic group, and often also to be welcoming and supportive towards birth parents.

Messages for policy and practice

- Permanent placement from care with foster and adoptive families not previously known to the child can be highly satisfactory for children and new parents of all ethnic groups.
- Even for the youngest group, permanent placement is not without risks, and supports designed around the needs of each family have to be built in from the start.

- It is important that, from the planning stage onwards, a 'sense of permanence' is encouraged in the foster parents as well as the children. There are many examples in the reports of how foster parents and social workers succeeded in doing this.

- Lessons can be learned from the African-Caribbean and South Asian parents in the study who had a particular capacity for empathy with the birth parents and for facilitating the continuing birth family contact that most of the children wanted.

Delivering Foster Care[15]

John Triseliotis
University of Edinburgh
Moira Walker and Malcolm Hill
Glasgow Centre for the Child & Society, University of Glasgow

The study reported here was funded by the Scottish Executive and carried out in Scotland between 1996 and 1998. It was prompted by concerns about the structure and organisation of the fostering services, and about the supply and retention of foster carers relative to the demand for them.

Study design

The policies, organisation, structures and service delivery systems of all 32 unitary authorities were studied by means of interviews and documentary analysis. The main part of the research was a postal questionnaire survey of current and former foster carers across Scotland. More than 800 foster carers (74% of those mailed) and almost 100 former foster carers (49% of those mailed) returned completed questionnaires. Further qualitative material was obtained through interviews and group discussions with 40 active and 27 former foster carers.

Key findings

STRUCTURE AND ORGANISATION

The fostering service had a firm place within the children and families division of almost all agencies. Three quarters of the agencies observed a clear delineation between workers responsible for foster carer support and those with case responsibility. In most agencies these two types of worker were operating from different locations and had separate line managers. In the majority of agencies the recruitment, approval and training of foster carers, along with carers' reviews, were centralised. Almost half the agencies had set up special schemes for adolescents, but these did not protect them against carer shortages. Only four per cent of children were fostered by voluntary/independent agencies.

POLICY MAKING ON FOSTER CARE

The profile of fostering within many local authorities was found to be low, adversely affecting policy development and resourcing. As a result long-term policy and strategic planning were hard to find. The contribution of foster carers, young people and parents to fostering policy making was either lacking or unsystematic. Existing and emerging new policies were failing to address some of the key limitations of the service perceived by carers, especially the inadequacies of the social work services offered to children.

THE RECRUITMENT, ASSESSMENT AND PREPARATION OF CARERS

A quarter of the agencies, especially those serving urban populations, reported experiencing serious carer shortages. Factors affecting recruitment and retention of carers were found to be closely linked, with carer satisfaction playing a crucial part in both. Campaigns to recruit new carers were largely one-off and unsystematic. In almost half the agencies budgetary constraints were also holding back recruitment campaigns. The most influential and successful recruitment methods were local in nature, especially word of mouth, feature articles and advertisements in the local press. Stressing the needs of local children was said to be productive. At the national level television was seen to have most influence. Carers stated that fears and stereotypes about fostering and social workers were holding back recruitment. Preparation and training were well received, but carers asked for more structured and more coherent forms of continued training.

ISSUES OF SUPPLY AND DEMAND

Around one household in every 900 were found to foster, but there were wide variations between agencies, with many urban authorities having the worst record. On average carers foster for seven years. Of those who ceased to foster almost three fifths gave reasons related to the operation of the fostering service, including the severity of the children's problems. Fears of false allegations of physical or sexual abuse occupied the minds of almost all carers. During the period 1996/97, 7 per cent of carers ceased to foster, well below common perceptions of heavy losses. Gains of new recruits over losses for the same period amounted to six per cent of all carers.

A census of referrals for placement revealed that over half the children were said to present behavioural and emotional problems. Around two fifths of them were members of sibling groups and one tenth of all referrals had a disability or health problem. Almost three out of every ten children referred for placement had remained unplaced because of a lack of a suitable placement. Another 14 per cent had gone to placements which were not a first choice. Hardest to place were black and Asian children (but few in actual numbers), children requiring long-term placements, offenders, children with disabilities and those displaying behavioural and emotional problems.

PLACEMENT WORKERS AND CHILDREN'S SOCIAL WORKERS

The placement (link) worker system operated by most agencies elicited high approval rates from foster carers, particularly for their responsiveness. They were seen to be more knowledgeable about childcare than children's social workers. Compared to placement staff based in area teams, those attached to placement units received significantly higher approval ratings from foster carers.

Almost seven out of every ten carers were satisfied with the operation of the fostering service overall. However, many identified major shortcomings and one in six was dissatisfied with almost all the activities of the children's social worker. The chief complaints centred on infrequent visits, unavailability, unreliability and lack of adequate support to carers and children. Poor availability and general support from the children's social worker was significantly associated with carers finding the children difficult, expectations not having been met, thinking about giving up fostering and actually doing so. Shortcomings of the children's social worker service were mainly attributed to resource limitations, to priority been given to child protection work and to the inadequate training of children's social workers.

FINANCIAL ARRANGEMENTS

Almost all the agencies were paying the basic child's maintenance allowance recommended by the then National Foster Care Association. A quarter were also paying a fee linked mostly to the child's age and to presenting difficulties. Carers drawing a fee were on the whole more satisfied with the operation of the fostering service. The multiplicity of payment schemes left many carers perplexed and confused, leading to calls for a national salaried service with immediate attention paid to the provision of occupational pensions to carers. The agencies received least approval from carers about their financial arrangements, especially as regards willingness to pay single grants and delays in payment.

Messages for policy and practice

The fostering service was found to have many strengths and this possibly explains the low number of foster carers leaving it each year. The problem is not so much one of loss, but one of recruiting and retaining carers for longer than the average of seven years. Nevertheless, the service was also facing some major challenges requiring authorities to:

- develop far more distinctive, detailed and long-term foster care policies
- raise the profile of the service
- significantly raise the quality of social worker support services to children and foster carers
- consider the provision of support to carers as central to the operation of the whole service
- establish much greater rapport with carers at all levels and make partnership a much greater reality than it is at present
- obtain annually objective feedback from carers who leave the service.

Testing the Limits of Foster Care: Fostering as an Alternative to Secure Accommodation[16]

Moira Walker
Social Work Research Centre, University of Stirling
Malcolm Hill
Glasgow Centre for the Child & Society, University of Glasgow
John Triseliotis
University of Strathclyde

The Community Alternative Placement Scheme (CAPS) was set up by NCH Action for Children (Scotland) in 1997 to provide foster care placements as an alternative to secure accommodation. Its evaluation was funded by the then Scottish Office and covered the first three years of the scheme's operation.

In Scotland, between 200 and 250 young people are admitted to secure accommodation each year, with about 90 in placement at any one time. A majority are boys, but about a quarter are girls. Girls are much more likely to be admitted for welfare reasons, rather than for offending. Approximately two thirds of young people in secure accommodation are placed there on the authority of a Children's Panel, because they are repeatedly running away and/or present a risk to themselves or other people. The remaining third are subject to a court order, either on remand or serving a sentence for a serious crime. The CAPS scheme catered only for young people placed by the Children's Panel.

CAPS built on developments in specialist fostering over the last 20 years, but was exceptional in its high fee levels and more comprehensive support arrangements. Core elements of the new service were to be:

- carer payments equivalent to a reasonable salary
- intensive support to carers, available 24 hours a day
- specialist training
- automatic entitlement to respite care (eight weeks per year)
- individualised programmes
- educational support
- time-limited placements.

Study design

The research aimed to assess the extent to which the scheme met its goals and to evaluate the impact of its work on the young people placed. Its purpose was to develop evidence-based under-standing of professional foster care's potential to provide a community alternative to secure place-ment. The study design included several key elements:

- It was *longitudinal*, so that changes were charted in the project's development and the first 20 young people placed by the scheme (ten girls and ten boys) were followed for two years after their placement started.
- It included *evaluation of outcomes* for the young people and a *'quasi-experimental'* aspect, through following a comparison sample of young people in secure care over a similar period.
- It involved *evaluating processes* in terms of project development and the fostering task.

Data were gathered from case records and interviews with young people, foster carers, CAPS staff, local authority social workers and managers. Young people's progress was assessed at three points on the basis of information about their current circumstances and participants' assessments.

Key findings

THE DEVELOPMENT OF THE SCHEME

In less than three years, CAPS became well established, with about a third of Scottish authorities having a child placed with the scheme at any one time. The geographical spread of carers and referring agencies meant it became usual for young people to be placed 30 miles or more from their home area. While this gave some young people a fresh start, it could also make it difficult to sustain links with their home area.

Twenty-three couples and five single women carers were recruited. More than half of the carers were new to foster care, but had relevant experience. Six men were main full-time carers. Because remuneration equated to a salary, CAPS attracted people who would not otherwise have considered fostering.

Most of the core elements of the scheme were implemented as planned. Carers received a high level of remuneration, training and support. They particularly valued the availability of 24-hour support and regular breaks (eight weeks in the year). Some indicated that the levels of payment and support had been crucial in encouraging them to persist at times of severe crisis. No carers left the scheme during its first three years of operation, nor did any carer insist on a placement ending against the wishes of the young person and social workers. There was on-going discussion between carers and staff about the level of risk which could be accommodated within a family home and the level of disruption to their family life which carers should be willing to tolerate.

In two key respects CAPS diverged from original plans:

- No educational support was provided within the scheme. This was a serious gap, especially since most young people required educational support and were placed outwith their home authority, where it was difficult to access specialist resources.

- Whereas the original intention was that placements would last for up to six months, several lasted up to two years, either because young people needed a longer period of stability or because there was no suitable provision for them to move on to.

The scheme continued to prioritise requests for placements for young people in secure accommodation, but also extended its scope. Of the young people included in the research, two thirds had been in or close to secure placement.

DID YOUNG PEOPLE BENEFIT?

Some young people benefited greatly, while for others the advantages were less clear. Benefits, in terms of developing confidence, skills and support systems, were highest for those who had been in placement for over a year and expected carers' support to continue after they left.

In contrast, over half (n = 14) of the first 20 placements ended prematurely without their goals being met. In most instances social workers and carers thought there had been benefits from the placement, but several of the endings were abrupt and traumatic. At the end of the study period, a number of young people still had no stable home base.

Over two years from the start of placements, outcomes were similar for young people placed with CAPS and those admitted to secure accommodation. Thus CAPS had achieved similar results without the loss of freedom or high costs associated with secure care.

When young people talked about the benefits of placements, they talked about how the carers had treated them and times they had enjoyed, rather than how they had progressed.

Messages for policy and practice

- With appropriate remuneration and support, the pool of foster carers can be increased and carers are able to care for very challenging young people.

- What foster care can offer depends not simply on the skill and commitment of carers and their employing agencies, but the availability of other services such as specialist education, mental health services and appropriately supportive accommodation and work for young people to move on to.

- Family placement does constitute a risk for older teenagers, so contingency plans should be in place to cater for the possibility of abrupt and premature endings.

The Advisory and Implementation Group

Note: The roles given are those held by the participants at the time.

Carolyn Davies	Chair, Senior Principal Research Liaison Officer, Department of Health and Social Security
Joanna Adande	Foster Carer and Membership Manager, Fostering Network
Celia Atherton	Implementation Lead, Director, Research in Practice
Christine Ballinger	Area Manager, Children and Families, Dudley Social Services Department
Jackie Daniel	Team Manager, Children and Families, West Berkshire Social Services Department
Mary Day	Training and Development Officer, Islington Social Services Department
Ronny Flynn	Lecturer (Children and Families), Open University
Anne Goldsmith	Assistant Director, Cheshire Social Services Department
Helen Jones	Inspector, Department for Education and Skills
Bridget Lindley	Legal Adviser, Family Rights Group
Peter McParlin	Educational Psychologist and Former Foster Child, Pupil and Parents Service, Harrogate
Kath Nelson	Assistant Director, Wigan Social Services Department
David Quinton	Professor of Psychosocial Development, University of Bristol
Clive Sellick	Senior Lecturer, University of East Anglia
Ian Sinclair	Review Author, Co-director of Social Work Research and Development Unit, University of York
Robert Tapsfield	Director, Fostering Network
Mick Upsall	Planning and Project Manager, Derbyshire Social Services Department
Pat Walton	Director of Children's and Family Services, Boys and Girls Welfare Society

References

1. Aldgate, J. and Bradley, M. (1999) *Supporting Families through Short-term Fostering.* London: The Stationery Office.

2. Cleaver, H. (2000) *Fostering Family Contact: A Study of Children, Parents and Foster Carers.* London: The Stationery Office.

3. Farmer, E., Moyers, S. and Lipscombe, J. (2004) *Fostering Adolescents.* London: Jessica Kingsley Publishers.

4. Hunt, J. *Family and Friends Carers.* Scoping paper presented for the Department of Health. *http://www.dfes.gov.uk/qualityprotects/pdfs/friends-family-paper.pdf*

5. Kirton, D., Beecham, J. and Ogilvie, K. (2004) 'Remuneration and Performance in Foster Care: Report to Department for Education and Skills.' Canterbury: University of Kent.

6. Macdonald, G. and Kakavelakis, I. (2004) 'Helping Foster Carers to Manage Challenging Behaviour: An Evaluation of a Cognitive-Behavioural Training Programme for Foster Carers.' Exeter: Centre for Evidence-Based Research, University of Exeter.

7. Quinton, D., Rushton, A., Dance, C. and Mayes, D. (1998) *Joining New Families: A Study of Adoption and Fostering in Middle Childhood.* Chichester: John Wiley.

8. Rushton, A., Dance, C., Quinton, D. and Mayes, D. (2001) *Siblings in Late Permanent Placements.* London: British Agencies for Adoption and Fostering.

9. Selwyn, J., Sturgess, W., Quinton, D. and Baxter, C. (2003) *Costs and Outcomes of Non-infant Adoptions: Report to the Department for Education and Skills.* London: DfES.

10. Sinclair, I., Gibbs, I. and Wilson, K. (2004) *Foster Carers: Why They Stay and Why They Leave.* London: Jessica Kingsley Publishers.

11. Sinclair, I., Gibbs, I. and Wilson, K. (2004) *Foster Placements: Why They Succeed and Why They Fail.* London: Jessica Kingsley Publishers.

12. Sinclair, I., Baker, C., Wilson, K. and Gibbs, I. (2004) *Foster Children: Where They Go and How They Get On.* London: Jessica Kingsley Publishers.

13. Skuse, T. and Ward, H. (2003) 'Listening to Children's Views of Care and Accommodation', Report to the Department of Heath. Loughborough: Centre for Child and Family Research, University of Loughborough.

14. Thoburn, J., Norford, L. and Parvez Rashid, S. (2000) *Permanent Family Placement for Children of Minority Ethnic Origin.* London: Jessica Kingsley Publishers.

15. Triseliotis, J., Walker, M. and Hill, M. (2000) *Delivering Foster Care.* London: British Agencies for Adoption and Fostering.

16. Walker, M., Hill, M. and Triseliotis, J. (2002) *Testing the Limits of Foster Care: Fostering as an Alternative to Secure Accommodation.* London: British Agencies for Adoption and Fostering.

17. Farmer, E. and Moyers, S. (forthcoming 2005) 'Children Placed with Relatives or Friends: Placement Patterns and Outcomes', Report to the Department for Education and Skills. Bristol: University of Bristol.

18. Farmer, E. and Pollock, S. (1998) *Sexually Abused and Sexually Abusing Children in Substitute Care.* Chichester: John Wiley.

19. Harwin, J., Owen, M., Locke, R. and Forrester, D. (2001) *Making Care Orders Work: A Study of Care Plans and their Implementation.* London: Stationery Office.

20. Lowe, N., Murch, M., with Bader, K., Borkowski, M., Copner, R., Lisles, C. and Shearman, J. (2001) *The Plan for the Child: Adoption or Long-term Fostering.* London: British Association for Adoption and Fostering.

21. Packman, J. and Hall, C. (1998) *From Care to Accommodation.* London: The Stationery Office.

22. Ward, H., Munro, E.R., Dearden, C. and Nicholson, D. (forthcoming 2005) *Care Experiences and Decision-Making for Very Young Children.* London: Jessica Kingsley Publishers.

23. Wilson, K., Sinclair, I., Taylor, C., Pithouse, A. and Sellick, C. (2004) *Fostering Success: An Exploration of the Research Literature on Foster Care.* London: Social Care Institute for Excellence.

24 Rowe, J. et al. (1985) *Social Work Decisions in Child Care: Recent Research Findings and their Implications.* London: HMSO.

Index

abuse
    allegations 111–12
    of children in birth families
        27, 29
    and contact with birth
        families 93, 156
    effects 51, 70–1
    emotional 70–1, 78, 79, 81,
        82, 95
    sexual 62, 70–1
admission to care, causes 26–7
adolescent fostering study 18,
    63–4, 84–5, 133–6
    and contact 89–90, 92–3, 95
    and education 97, 98, 99
    foster carer stresses 104, 105
    and foster families 77, 80, 82,
        83
    leaving care outcomes 31
    and placement 60, 62, 65, 69,
        71, 72
    and support 109–10, 111–12
adolescents
    behavioural problems 69
    characteristics 134
    contact with birth families
        89–90, 91, 92–3, 149
    needs 52
    placement
        breakdown 63–4, 68, 70,
            71, 82
        consultation on 62, 63,
            64
        outcomes 134–5, 156
        pressures on carers 84–5,
            105, 134–5
        stability 31
        success factors 63, 64, 82,
            134, 135
    research overview 133–6
    see also care leavers;
        independent living
adoption
    and age 32, 33, 155
    by foster carers 46, 140, 149
    characteristics of children
        148, 159
    costs 149
    delays 32, 148–9
    of ethnic minority children
        159–61
    and loss of support 46
    outcomes 29, 33, 45, 46,
        148, 149–50, 155, 156,
        157, 160

recommendations 123, 124,
    150, 157
research overviews 142–4,
    145–7, 148–50, 159–61
views of foster children 33,
    45–6
adoption study 19, 32, 33, 35, 45,
    46, 148–50
    and admission to care 27
    foster care outcomes 30, 31,
        33, 45
    and leaving care 29, 30
    and placement 64
    and relative foster care 43
    and support 54
adoptive parents
    information for 61–2
    support for 116–17, 149
    views on placement 61
age
    and behavioural problems 27,
        68–9
    and chance of adoption 32,
        33, 155
    effect on contact 89–90
    and fostering principles 124
    and placement breakdown 68,
        78
    and stability in care 31
Aldgate, J. see shared care study
allegations, of abuse 111–12
aspirations, of foster children
    50–1, 156
assessment
    of adoptive parents 61
    of children 35, 59, 65, 66,
        146, 150
attachment, development of 33,
    51, 81
authoritative parenting 80–1

Baker, C. see York study 3
Baxter, C. see adoption study
Beecham, J. see remuneration and
    performance study
behavioural problems
    and age 27, 68–9
    and carer stress 82–3
    causation 25
    likelihood of change 69
    management of 81, 83
    and placement breakdown
        68–9, 70
    research overview 141–2
    on returning home 29
    and specialist foster care 40–1
    statistics 27
    training for carers 83, 141–2

see also sexually abused
    children; training study
birth families
    abuse of children in 27, 29
    characteristics 26–7, 128
    contact with children see
        contact
    support for 40, 116–17, 123,
        128–9, 157
    see also parents; siblings
black children, importance of
    school 97
Bradley, M. see shared care study

CAPS project see specialist
    fostering study
care leavers 29, 53, 55, 98, 99
    see also independent living;
        returning home
care plans 59, 62, 111
    see also educational plans
carer groups 109
challenging behaviour see
    behavioural problems
child abuse see abuse
children see adolescents; ethnic
    minority children; foster
    children; foster families, birth
    children; sexually abused
    children; siblings
children's services
    Government initiatives 17
    see also foster care
choice
    need for 50, 54
    see also consultation
Cleaver, H. see contact study
coherence, need for 54–5
Community Alternatives
    Placement Scheme see
    specialist fostering study
consultation
    with children 55, 56
        about placement 62, 63,
            65–6, 131
        and placement success 64
        research overview 157–9
        see also choice
    with parents 62, 63, 94, 131
contact
    with birth families
        and abuse 93, 156
        by adolescents 89–90, 91,
            92–3, 149
        by adopted children 33,
            149
        aims 90–1
        benefits 89, 93, 95

social workers, support *cont.*
    for carers 84–5, 105,
      106–8, 109–14,
      116–17, 133–4,
      140, 149, 162
    for contact 131, 135
    for relative carers 104,
      106–7, 137, 138
    views on independent living
      30
    see also night duty teams;
      teamwork
Special Guardianship 33, 47
    see also residence orders
specialist foster care
    advantages 118
    and birth families 157
    carer turnover 113
    good practice 80
    needs of children 52
    outcomes 40–1, 165
    research overview 40–2,
      163–5
    and school 69, 97, 99, 165
    and training for carers 83
specialist fostering study 19,
    40–2, 163–5
    and contact 91–2
    and education 60, 69, 97, 98
    and foster families 80, 83
    and placement 61, 65
    and support 110, 113
    what children want/need 51,
      52
stability of care 29, 30–2, 44
    see also placement, success;
      placement breakdown
Sturgess, W. *see* adoption study
subjective permanence 32
supervised contact 131
supervising social workers *see*
    social workers
Supporting Families through
    Short-term Fostering *see*
    shared care study

teamwork 111
teenagers *see* adolescents
Testing the Limits of Foster Care
    see specialist fostering study
Thoburn, J. *see* East Anglia study
through care 29, 31, 38–40, 42,
    64, 65, 95, 156, 157
    see also families for life
training study 19, 52, 83, 116,
    141–2
    see also foster carers, training

transracial placements 73–4, 160
treatment foster care *see* specialist
    foster care
Triseliotis study 19, 101–4,
    118–19, 161–3
    and contact 92, 112
    foster carer stresses 104–5
    and foster families 77, 78
    and relative foster care 43
    and support 107, 108, 109,
      110, 111
    and training 115–16
    see also specialist fostering
      study
turnover of foster carers 104, 113
    see also recruitment

uncontested permanence 32

venues, for contact with birth
    families 91, 94, 131

Walker, M. *see* specialist fostering
    study; Triseliotis study
Ward, H. *see* Loughborough
    consumer study
Wilson, K. *see* York studies
working carers 106, 108–9

York study 1 (carers) 19, 107–9,
    150–2
    and ethnicity 74
    foster carer stresses 104–5,
      112
    and foster families 77, 80–1
    and recruitment 101, 102
    and relative foster care 42–3
    and support 106, 107,
      108–9, 110, 111, 119
York study 2 (placements) 19, 31,
    54, 60, 63, 68, 69, 70,
    152–4
    and contact 89, 90, 92, 93
    and disability 71, 72
    and education 98, 99
    and ethnicity 73
    and foster families 57, 77, 78,
      79–81, 82, 83
    and leaving care 27
    and placement breakdown 53,
      64, 79
    and relative foster care 44
    and support 85, 110, 119
    and training 117–18
    what children want/need 33,
      50–1

York study 3 (follow-up) 19,
    154–7
    and adoption 32, 33, 45–6
    and behavioural problems 69
    and contact 92, 93, 94
    and education 97, 98,
      99–100
    foster care outcomes 30,
      31–2, 33, 35, 45
    and foster families 80–1
    and leaving care 25, 28,
      29–30, 31, 35, 39, 55
    and placement 61–2, 64, 68,
      72, 73–4
    and short breaks 38, 39
    and support 40, 85, 116,
      117, 119
    what children want/need 27,
      50–1, 53

Printed in the United Kingdom
by Lightning Source UK Ltd.
136275UK00001B/53-90/P